FEB 1975
RECEIVED
OHIO DOMINICAN
COLLEGE LIBRARY
COLUMBUS, OHIO
43219

53-26

THE AFRICAN PHENOMENON

THE

AFRICAN

PHENOMENON

Abdul A. Said
The American University

ALLYN AND BACON, INC.
Boston, Massachusetts

320.096
S132a
1968

© Copyright 1968 by Allyn and Bacon, Inc., 470 Atlantic Avenue, Boston. All rights reserved. No part of this book may be reproduced in any form, or by any means, without permission in writing from the publisher.

Library of Congress Catalog Number 68-17286

PRINTED IN THE UNITED STATES OF AMERICA

Second printing . . . May, 1969

To the memory of
Charles O. Lerche

93587

AFRICA

POLITICAL DIVISIONS

★ Capital

BOUNDARY REPRESENTATION IS
NOT NECESSARILY AUTHORITATIVE

0   500   1000 MILES
0   500 1000 KILOMETERS

54825 10-66

Source: Bureau of Geographer, Department of State, Washington, D.C.

• Preface

Because so many books on Africa have been published in recent years, it is necessary to justify this undertaking.

To this analysis of the African phenomenon I bring a background of non-Western birth and American academic training in political science. In the past six years I have made several long and short trips throughout East, North, West and Central Africa. My role in Africa ranged from Rockefeller research scholar to American Specialist for the U.S. Department of State.

During these visits I lectured in almost every major institution of higher learning in independent Africa. I have discussed foreign policy issues and the problems of nation-building with Africans from various walks of life. Having observed the realities of what are usually referred to as "underdeveloped" states of the world — sometimes euphemistically categorized as "emerging" or "developing" states — I became increasingly aware that there is a wide gulf between image and realities in prevalent thinking about Africa.

The present confrontation between the modern, developed West and Africa has brought face to face hundreds of millions of whites, "natives" of the traditional international system, and blacks, "intruders" to the system. Both "natives" and "intruders" speak a language unintelligible to one another, yet both speak ever more loudly in an effort to make themselves known.

Scholars and diplomats of the West are engaged in a massive attempt to understand the nature of Africa. They have produced increasingly provocative studies and have advanced a cacophony of exotic theories on the "African mystique." Yet, in trying to understand the continent, both men of learning and men of action are discouraged by the striking disproportion between effort and reward.

Though vastly impressed by the excitement of the African adventure, many well-meaning American liberals have failed to serve their subject matter well. On one hand, they have led the public to expect too much of the fledgling states; on the other, they have been too quick to forgive the excessive African indulgence in what might be called "political cannibalism."

Americans must recognize the contradictions inherent in the double standards which they so readily apply in their comparative view of Africa and their own country. Logically, a sincere concern for civil rights and civil liberties in the United States should be matched by an equivalent concern for individual freedoms in Africa. One would expect the general attitude of anti-extremism in the United States to have its parallel in some degree of reservation about African extremism. Black supremacy in Africa should not be ignored by the liberal opponents of white supremacy in the United States. To continue to apply double standards and dual practices is to engage in a strange sort of intellectual witchcraft in which the "uncivilized" nations are scarcely judged at all.

At the other extreme, many American conservatives see nothing of value coming out of independent Africa. They readily condemn contemporary African growing pains as incurable diseases. They regard the African as totally incapable of controlling his own political destiny.

This book considers Africa as a unified phenomenon. While it recognizes that Africa is a continent of manifold diversities, it stresses the common denominators of independent Africa. The emphasis on patterns and theories, however, must not do violence to the facts. While the men and events that I have chosen as illustrations of theories are few in number, I believe that they reflect the African reality.

I have not attempted to analyze the international relations of the African states. Rather, I have attempted to examine the implications of the presence of an independent Africa in world affairs by raising the following issues: How will the international system respond to the impact of Africa? How will Africa act to fit itself, find its place, and, in general, adapt itself to an essentially Western international system? In other words, I have sought to determine whether the traditional international system will become appreciatively different as a result of the impact of Africa, or whether Africa will find it necessary to become more and more Western.

I acknowledge gratefully the board of the *Washington Evening Star* for its generous grant which has enabled me to complete my research. To my friends in Africa and the United States who have helped me and urged me to complete this book I owe a great debt. M'Kean M. Tredway assisted in every possible way through all stages of the book's preparation. Lee S. Houchins edited the manuscript with thoroughness and good cheer. William F. Ahlstrom and Richard M. Fraenkel were a source of data and inspiration. Professor Bahram Farzanegan of Asheville-Biltmore College shared with me his ideas and insights on American scholarship on the non-West. Anne Kopf was a faithful critic and inspired many ideas. George Harpootlian prepared the appendices. Stanley Frosh encouraged me to complete the manuscript. Finally, my family, with its toleration and comfort, sustained me at every stage of writing.

Abdul A. Said

✦ Contents

Map

1 **The Study of Africa and the Non-West**   1
   Development of Scholarship   2
   Approach of this Study   8

2 **The Impact of the International System upon Africa**   15
   Forces of Change in the International System   17
   The Impact of Change upon Africa   19
   The Evolving International System   22

3 **Problems of Continuity and Change**   29
   The Tribal Base   30
   The Religious Base   31
   The Colonial Legacy   35
   European Colonial Philosophies • *The Alienated Elites*
   The Search for New Values   42

4 **Contemporary African Revolutionary Thought**   47
   African Ambivalence   47
   Illustrations of African Revolutionary Thought   49
   Frantz Fanon • *Kwame Nkrumah* • *Gamal Abdel Nasser* • *Habib Bourguiba* • *Julius Nyerere* • *Ahmed Sékou Touré* • *Felix Houphouet-Boigny*
   One-Party Systems   61
   Apparent Directions of African Revolutionary Thought   65

5 **Freedom through Nationalism**   69
   The Nature of African Nationalism   70
   Anti-Colonialism   72
   Illustrations of African Nationalism   75
   Kwame Nkrumah • *Gamal Abdel Nasser* • *Habib*

Bourguiba • Jomo Kenyatta • Leopold Senghor
African Nationalism: An Assessment   83

6   **Progress through Socialism**   90
    The Nature of African Socialism   90
    Illustrations of African Socialism   93
    *Jomo Kenyatta • Leopold Senghor • Kwame
    Nkrumah • Gamal Abdel Nasser • Habib Bour-
    guiba*
    The Prospects for African Socialism   103

7   **Order through Pan-Africanism**   108
    Evolution of Pan-Africanism   110
    Origins • Emergence of Pan-African Groupings
    The Organization of African Unity (OAU)   120
    Pan-Africanism: An Assessment   123

8   **Security through Neutralism**   128
    The African Image of International Politics   129
    The Functions of Non-Alignment   132
    The Myth of the "Afro-Asian Bloc"   137
    Non-Alignment: An Assessment   139

9   **Africa's Impact upon the International System**   144
    The Ideologies of African Uniqueness   145
    The African System   150
    A View of the Future   156

Appendices   161
    A. Vital Statistics of the African States   161
    B. African Membership in Principal Regional and
        International Organizations and Conferences   164
    C. Charter of the Organization of African Unity   167
    D. Final Communiqué of the Asian-African Confer-
        ence, Bandung, April 24, 1955   176

Index

THE AFRICAN PHENOMENON

1 ◆

The Study of Africa
and the Non-West

The so-called "West," long the supreme arbiter of global politics, is now confronted with the emergence on the international political scene of a growing number of states whose history, tradition, and system of beliefs and values differ widely from the common heritage of those nations which are considered, in the broadest sense, as belonging to the Western world. The term "non-West" as used here is not a geographical designation but includes rather all parts of the world that have in common their difference from the West, their newness to the international scene, and their need to assert themselves as states and to find a place in an international political system which has only recently begun to make room for them. More specifically, "non-West" refers here to those states that have acquired their independence since the Second World War. Nowhere have more radical and rapid changes been made during this period than in the continent of Africa.

In the past two decades, the new African states have managed to establish themselves as an influential factor in international politics. In response to this recently acquired position of importance considerable inquiry has been directed to the problems of African modernization and nation-building. Prior to the Second World

War, political literature on Africa consisted primarily of the memoirs of missionaries and colonial administrators. The more recent studies of Africa and the non-Western world have, however, been characterized by the utilization of a broad spectrum of analytical approaches and research techniques.

DEVELOPMENT OF SCHOLARSHIP

Prior to and immediately following the Second World War, popular notions of underdevelopment were dominated by a stereotyped image of the non-Western states. A given state was considered to be underdeveloped if it failed to fit a model structured by Western notions of politics, economics, and community; if the state lacked democratic, competitive political parties and a high standard of living, it was, by definition, underdeveloped. Few scholars gave serious thought to the dynamic nature of the modernization process, and it was generally believed that a people emerging from colonialism would naturally express their independence in a systematic effort toward the construction of a modern nation-state. To some extent, Afro-Asians accepted this interpretation and shared with Westerners the simplistic view that traditional societies could be immediately refashioned on the modern, Western model.

This optimistic approach was reflected in the few early postwar analyses of the non-West. These were largely historical, administrative, and anthropological studies. Historians were generally preoccupied with the origin and evolution of particular states. Political scientists were engaged in comparative analyses of newly formed constitutional, electoral, and legislative processes, and employed the conceptual baggage of the Western political tradition. Perhaps alone among the social scientists, anthropologists rejected the normative patterns of thought that characterized most of the studies produced in this initial period. Inveterate defenders of cultural values, they upheld a relativistic ethic which opposed, at least by implication, the inflicting of alien rule on weaker societies. However, because of their commitment to cultural empathy, few anthropologists managed to contribute very much to the understanding of the modernization process.[1]

Because the early transitional period in the non-West was characterized by stubbornly persisting political instability and social discontinuity, Western scholars' early enthusiasm for independence and happy anticipation of seeing non-Western states evolve along modern democratic lines began to fade. The disappointingly unrestrained revolutionary momentum and the attendant turmoil that persisted led to a re-examination of prior assumptions. Some observers attributed such difficulties to an international communist conspiracy. Others viewed them as the inevitable consequence of premature independence.[2] Using such indices as per capita income, literacy rates, and levels of industrialization, economists and sociologists associated political with economic backwardness. Some emphasized the need for economic and military assistance to countries threatened by communist aggression and infiltration. Setting aside their normative attitudes, political scientists often limited their approach to the context of the cold war. As the U.S.-U.S.S.R. rivalry intensified, the practice of international development and alternative approaches to the problems of modernization (communist vs. democratic) acquired considerable status as important foreign policy issues.

With the organization of the International Co-operation Administration in 1955, there was a marked acceleration in the growth of the entire body of development literature. Primarily descriptive and often oratorical, these studies usually dealt with the economic and procedural aspects of modernization. There were few attempts to analyze the problems of modernization within a theoretical framework. Western social scientists were reluctant to think about the issues of modernization in a meaningful pattern. Having conceived of the problem in terms of the unprecedented speed and intensity of social change, they found it difficult to make explicit hypotheses or to relate theory to specific issues. However, the resulting concern with modernization problems as issues in themselves had the salutary effect of forcing social scientists to devise new categories and techniques for analysis of the phenomena of rapid social and political change.

One outgrowth of this trend was a revolution in the social sciences.[3] Like the independence of new states from colonial rule, the liberation of the social sciences from the restrictive normative approach was a post-war development. And it was equally beset by anarchy and confusion. Many of the theoretical and methodological innovations in the social sciences rivalled in degree, if not in intensity, the parochial nature of the nationalism of emerging states. In many ways, the scholars who concentrated on the underdeveloped areas often appeared to be more interested in the states of their disciplines than in the state of the non-Western world.[4]

Nonetheless, as a result of the increasing use of comparative analysis techniques and of crossdisciplinary and interdisciplinary co-operation, there was widespread optimism that research on the non-West stood on the threshold of considerable achievement. Students of the non-West began to devote themselves to methodologies and the construction of developmental theories which produced useful predictive hypotheses. Captivated by the notions of predictability, political scientists were most ambitious in this area of inquiry.[5] This optimism was also reflected in the more recent growth of functional and behavioral theories which attempt to relate political and governmental institutions to other dimensions of the social system. This trend was further evident in the development of the so-called dynamic theories of the future political evolution of the non-Western world.[6]

Social scientists integrated the sociological, economic, and political theories and methodologies focusing on the emerging states. During the past few years, scholars and policymakers in the United States have become increasingly interested in this new approach. It originated with the general need for research on economic development and related problems of foreign aid administration. At the same time, political scientists proclaimed that their discipline was overburdened with narrow and often perfunctory approaches to development problems. It was felt, in particular, that a combined and comprehensive social science approach was necessary to assess and order the phenomena of rapid social change in environments of astonishing diversity and variety. Only in this way, it was argued, could knowledge of the modernization process be broadened and valid generalizations be developed.[7]

This combined effort toward a deeper understanding of non-Western political development, as contrasted with the exclusively technical problems of economic development, is regarded as one of the most significant advances in social science research on emerging states. Resting on the assumption that a significant relationship exists between social, economic, and political development, this approach has been praised for giving the policymaker a fresh and more realistic method of assessing the long-range problems of development.

Because of the often extreme difficulties encountered by Afro-Asians in building modern, politically viable entities out of their traditional societies, the primary importance of political socialization was recognized as the key to the over-all process of modernization.[8] It is now generally assumed that political development is a precondition of fully successful economic development. Accordingly, social scientists have attempted to analyze the problem systematically by converging on theoretical and methodological interests.[9] The fact that political scientists use such terms as "legitimacy," "stability," "adaption," "articulation," "aggregation," rather than "constitutions," "elections," "interest groups," and "legislatures" is indicative of the shift toward functional and behavioral theory.

This new method of inquiry, it is claimed, provides the analyst with insights into political systems characterized by unstable institutions and groups that perform differently from those in the more stable, and more familiar, Western societies.[10] New classifications and typologies serve as the building blocks of new theories and, ultimately, provide predictive hypotheses on the political evolution of the non-West.

A prime mover in this search for an understanding of political development was the Committee on Comparative Politics of the Social Science Research Council.[11] In an endeavor to analyze the significance of political change in the developing and developed countries, Committee social scientists collected world-wide data to test the hypothesis that states which enjoy a high degree of urbanization, education, industrialization, and wealth, tend to be stable and democratic. From these investigations, a theoretical framework was constructed and applied to six areas of the world. The Committee's findings indicate that a "positive correlation exists between economic development and political competitiveness."[12]

As one direct consequence of the functional and behavioral theory, assorted models of underdeveloped countries are being constructed by anthropologists, psychologists, economists, and sociologists, with a view toward contributing to a deeper understanding of political development. Scholars in these disciplines assert certain, not necessarily valid, causal relationships.[13]

Economists, for example, utilize a multitude of readily available, objectively quantifiable criteria. These include gross national product, per capita income, rates of economic growth, and outputs of electricity. Countries are classified according to obvious economic indicators, and the degree of "progress," if any, is measured.[14] In contrast, the assessment of political development is a difficult and highly complicated undertaking. The most fundamental difficulty concerns the criteria of development. There is no agreement regarding what constitutes a "developed" polity. Most descriptions of political development are, indeed, value-laden. The "advanced" Western standards employed in the measurement of political development are, in themselves, either dubious or controversial. Comparisons between the developed and underdeveloped sectors of the world are generally made on the basis of Western norms and values.

Another difficulty arises from incomplete understanding of the political processes in emerging states. Investigations of these processes are frequently based on the interpretations expounded by Afro-Asian elites. But, because they tend to be emotionally and intellectually preoccupied with the broader issues of imperialism, residual colonialism, neo-colonialism, pan-ism, and the like, the Afro-Asian elites have seldom provided the Western scholars with an objective appraisal of internal factors relevant to the local political process.

However, as a beneficial by-product of the behavioral approach, such informational deficiencies are being gradually reduced; scientific method requires the intensive analysis of social units and social problems of limited scope.

But, if the problem is to be approached in terms of political structure, no particular model can be claimed to represent a necessary or ideal type of economic and social development. Even in the present century, advanced Western states have experimented with or accepted divergent governmental institutions. These have ranged from monarchies to multi-party democracies, from oligarchic capitalism to democratic centralism.[15] It has been argued also that the new and emerging states may require innovative forms of governmental institutions, perhaps related to their own societal values and traditions.[16]

Western analysis of the non-West often begins with the proposition that a corollary of social and economic conditions among emerging states is a discrete mode of political development. Despite the improvement in analytical methods and techniques, the problem is often approached with unconsciously implied normative definitions. The most popular approaches are based on the assumption that democracy is a synonym of modernity, that it is the ideal form of political development, and that it is a pre-requisite of development.[17] But democracy has produced so many hybrids and derivations, and is applied to such a multitude of aphorisms, that it has lost its meaning—unless precisely defined within the organic framework of the given state. Such value-laden definitions and approaches to the problems of political development are currently criticized or challenged by Afro-Asians who reject many Western norms and standards as irrelevant to their experience. In rejecting Western competitive democracy, Afro-Asian politicans and elites claim that more relevant political ideals and "realities" are to be found within their own traditional societies.

Some prominent American political scientists have sought to integrate the ideas of system, culture, function, structure, and action in a conceptual scheme particularly designed for comparative analysis. This approach is an obvious improvement on the narrower and more provincial studies of political behavior; it avoids petty inquiries into voting behavior, legislation, and other rituals of democratism. It seeks to identify and analyze the politico-cultural systems and sub-systems in states at any level of political sophistication. Its method of inquiry, relying on sociological and anthropological theory, rejects the earlier separation of comparative politics into East-West, American, African, Middle Eastern area studies. This approach advocates an empirical analysis of political functions and the processes of change and modernization without regard to cultural or geographical peculiarities. Because of its more precise analytical framework, the behavioral approach has provided a strengthened conceptual unity in the study of comparative politics. But, at the same time, the behavioral approach has minimized the importance of values and goals by placing its primary emphasis on *processes*. So far, its methods have prevented significant treatment of the subjective dimensions of modernization.[18]

It is conceded that behavioral methods of research enable political scientists to construct refined inventories, detailed charts, and useful models of the political system. Quantitative analysis yields sophisticated information on the distribution and composition of the national political body as a means for testing hypotheses.

However, the question remains whether the behavioralists' scattered interest in such a variety of analytical methods and their grandiose display of statistical data provide meaningful results. All too often, a great deal of effort is expended in confirming previous—and rather obvious—expectations. In their attempt to analyze all political systems in terms of one universally applicable set of concepts, on one hand, they confound realities with concepts; on the other hand, they ignore existent realities. By dismissing the traditional political concepts of rule, authority, and power, behavioralism has smothered political science in a psychological —or, more frequently, sociological—wet blanket. By adopting a battery of "unifying" concepts, the behavioralist attempts to refocus political science on non-political objects.

One unfortunate consequence of this new approach has been the attempt to understand political relations in terms of consensus rather than power and coercion. Unfortunately, most general theories of political development are crippled by the invalid assumption that the consensual model is the only useful model of advanced political behavior and that the underdeveloped countries remain so because they have failed to achieve political integration.

The behavioralist bases his generalization on distinct societal types. He distinguishes the integrative from the coercive society: the first is based upon moral order or consensus; the second involves elements of power, interests, coercion, change, and conflict.[19] It is more useful to view societies as combinations of integrative and coercive types.

It is evident that, as an unhappy consequence of the recent and contemporary emphasis on behavioral methodologies, the study of international relations in the United States is culture-bound. The "New Scientism" is deeply colored by the American experience and relies overmuch on extrapolation from American norms.[20] This is the central weakness of contemporary American studies on African and non-Western politics.

APPROACH OF THIS STUDY

Our approach consists in identifying the skeletal structure of the political modernization process. The basic qualification of a "modern" state is the ability to live, to produce, and to organize in a fashion which satisfies the needs and aspirations of its society.[21] On a higher level of generalization, the most trust-worthy indices of the success or failure of any political system—Western or non-Western—can be abstracted from the advances made toward the goal of need-satisfaction. The maintenance of internal order and the preservation of the state's external security are minimal, if not fundamental, requirements. But the aspirations of ruling elites in the new and emerging states frequently extend far beyond the boundaries of the aspirations of their own people.

For some of the emerging states, a major source of difficulty, and even potential disaster, is the absence of any kind of national solidarity. The broad gap between old and new, modern and pre-modern, and radical and conservative elements of society forms a formidable barrier to political transition. The ultimate result is permanent disjuncture between the cosmopolitan and the local, the literate and the illiterate, and the rulers and the ruled. National unity is further impeded by the divisive effects of the incorporation of differing racial, tribal, caste, religious, and lin-guistic communities within a single political framework. When substantial sectors of the population are barely aware of the exist-ence of either the state or its government, it is nearly impossible to enlist the active participation of the people in the creation of a viable state, much less to set in motion the processes of economic development. For this reason, Afro-Asian political leaders have continually emphasized domestic unity, the symbols of sovereignty and independence, and enlargement of the state apparatus. But even though the social and political integration of diverse elements demands first priority, the Afro-Asian states have assumed the broader task of seeking to exercise power and influence as active participants in the international system.

In view of the conditions described above, it is intellectually hazardous to undertake the establishment of a definitive relation-ship between the social, economic, and political factors of change in the contemporary non-Western world. However satisfying it might be to construct a theoretical relationship among such com-plex factors in an attempt to predict the patterns of non-Western political evolution, such an enterprise contributes little of value to the fuller understanding of the constantly changing political processes of the non-West.

The problem of political development must be approached in a less grand manner. As suggested above, a more useful method of inquiry would be to determine to what extent the minimum requirements of political modernization are met by means and practices actually employed in a given context.

This study applies a similar method of analysis to the African context. It is an attempt to cut away, or at least to de-emphasize, some of the more misleading generalities employed by contemporary Africans in their search for identity. It also seeks to place the questions of particular African national destinies in a more accurate historical perspective. This study then examines the extent of Africa's preparation for the task of adapting to contemporary revolutionary conditions, the underlying assumptions and postulates of contemporary African revolutionary thought, African attitudes toward the process of change, the problem of direction in African history, and the concept of the nature of the African personality. It argues that African revolutionary thought is characterized by four basic concepts: the pursuit of freedom through nationalism, progress through socialism, order through Pan-Africanism, and security through neutralism or non-alignment. Each of these concepts is treated in depth and is illustrated by analyses of its principal political proponents.

Finally, it considers the implications of the emergence of Africa—and the attendant response of both the Africans themselves and the entire international system.

NOTES

1. For an excellent study of the role of an anthropologist and the problems of modernization, see Sidney W. Mintz, "Anthropologist and Development: Cultural Relativism and the Making of Policy" (Paper presented to the American Sociological Association, 5th Annual Meeting, August 31—September 3, 1964; Montreal, Canada). Mintz argues that an anthropologist less frequently weighs the benefits derived from technical improvements, thus losing one of anthropology's basic contentions: Culture and integrated systems—change in one institution usually brings change in others.

2. This minority opinion was held by former colonial administrators, and was later to become popularly accepted after the Congo fiasco in 1960. For an earlier view see James S. Coleman, *Nigeria: Background to Nationalism* (Berkeley, Calif.: University of California

Press, 1958), p. 193, quoted by Sir Hugh Clifford, Governor of Nigeria (1920): "The suggestion that there is or can be in the visible future such a thing as an African nation is as manifest an absurdity as there is or can be until the arrival of the Millennium." For a reevaluation of premature independence, see Colin Legum, *Congo Disaster* (Baltimore, Md.: Penguin Books, 1961).

3. For a comprehensive study on the nature of current and prospective social research on the developing areas, see for example, Robert A. Lystad (ed.), *The African World: A Survey of Social Research* (New York: Frederick A. Praeger, 1965). See also, Leonard Binder, "National Integration and Political Development," (Paper delivered at the annual meeting of the American Political Science Association in September, 1963).

4. This is characterized by a plethora of theoretical analyses devoted to "long-range" problems, social structures, functions, etc. See for example, Robert E. Asher *et al.*, *Development of the Emerging Countries: An Agenda for Research* (Washington, D. C.: The Brookings Institution, 1962); and Karl W. Deutsch, "Social Mobilization and Political Development," *American Political Science Review*, LV (September, 1961), 493-514.

5. Prime movers in the search for an understanding of "political development" from an integrated theoretical social science approach for the purpose of establishing predictive hypothesis, see the now classical study, Gabriel A. Almond and James S. Coleman (eds.), *Politics of the Developing Areas* (Princeton, N.J.: Princeton University Press, 1960). See also the study by Gabriel A. Almond, "Political Systems and Political Change," *American Behavorial Scientist*, X (June, 1963), 3-10.

6. A good illustration of the predilection for prediction is David Horowitz, "Economic Development and Democracy," *Journal of International Affairs*, XVI (1962), 183-190.

7. Robert A. Dahl, "The Behavioral Approach: Epitaph to a Monument to a Successful Protest," *The American Political Science Review*, LV (December, 1961), 763-772.

8. Taylor P. Ostrander, "Problems of African Development," *Orbis*, IV (Summer, 1960), 192-194. See also, Almond, *loc. cit.* By presenting a typology of socio-governmental forms, Almond ties together the traditional and newer concerns in the study of political behavior.

9. This is particularly applicable to current social science research on Africa. See Lystad (ed.), *op. cit.*

10. Philip Cutright, "National Political Development: Measurement and Analysis," *American Sociological Review*, XXVIII (April,

1963), 253-256. This presents a classification of states according to degree of democratic political development and a statistical index of development.

11. Almond and Coleman (eds.), *op. cit.*

12. The conclusions themselves are not startling; the same inference was made earlier by S. M. Lipset, *Political Man* (Garden City, N.Y.: Doubleday and Company, Inc., 1960). He suggested that states with a high index of education, urbanization, etc., tend to be stable and democratic. Almond and Coleman only cast this notion in a theoretical hypothesis, using much of his material in the process.

13. John H. Adler, "Some Policy Problems in Economic Development," *Economic Development and Cultural Change,* IX (January, 1961), 111-112.

14. Walt W. Rostow, *The Stages of Economic Growth* (New York: Cambridge University Press, 1960).

15. Rupert Emerson, "Nationalism and Political Development," *Journal of Politics,* XXII (January, 1960), 3-11. Also, "Political Modernization: The Single Party System," (Monograph No. 1, 1963-1964, published by the University of Denver Monograph Series in World Affairs), 5-6. This presents a succinct evaluation of political modernization.

16. This view is gaining currency as reflected in John H. Kautsky (ed.), *Political Change in Underdeveloped Countries* (New York: John Wiley and Sons, 1962). See also, Immanuel Wallerstein, *Africa: The Politics of Independence* (New York: Vintage Books, 1961), an essay which recognizes this possibility by emphasizing traditional values in terms of political development.

17. Horowitz, *loc. cit.;* Lipset, *op. cit.,* describes the social conditions which exist for democracy to survive, with emphasis on the types of environment which support or threaten existing democratic institutions. Joseph Spangle, "Economic Development: Political Preconditions," *Journal of Politics,* XXII (August, 1960), 378, is among only the few studies which start with this presupposition.

18. See Gabriel A. Almond and G. Bingham Powell Jr., *Comparative Politics, a Developmental Approach* (Boston: Little, Brown and Co., 1966).

19. See Edward Shils, "On the Comparative Study of the New States," in Clifford Geertz's *Old Societies and New States* (New York: The Free Press of Glencoe, 1963).

20. Barrington Moore, *Political Power and Social Theory* (New York: Harper and Row, 1965), 89-110.

21. Emerson, "Political Modernization: The Single-Party System," *op. cit.,* 4.

BIBLIOGRAPHY

ALMOND, GABRIEL and COLEMAN, JAMES S. (eds.) *Politics of the Developing Areas.* Princeton, N.J.: Princeton University Press, 1960.

ANDERSON, CHARLES W. *et al. Issues of Political Development.* Englewood Cliffs, N.J.: Prentice-Hall, 1967.

APTER, DAVID. *The Politics of Modernization.* Chicago: University of Chicago Press, 1965.

ASHER, ROBERT E. *et al. Development of the Emerging Countries: An Agenda for Research.* Washington, D.C.: The Brookings Institution, 1962.

BRAIBANTI, RALPH and SPENGLER, JOSEPH J. (eds.). *Tradition, Values and Socio-Economic Development.* Durham, N.C.: Duke University Press, 1961.

ECKSTEIN, HARRY and APTER, DAVID E. (eds.). *Comparative Politics.* New York: The Free Press of Glencoe, 1963.

EISENSTADT, SAMUEL N. *The Political Systems of Empires.* New York: The Free Press of Glencoe, 1963.

EMERSON, RUPERT. "Political Modernization: The Single-Party System" (Monograph No. 1, 1963-64, published by the University of Denver for the Monograph Series in World Affairs).

FARRELL, R. BARRY (ed.). *Approaches to Comparative and International Politics.* Evanston, Ill.: Northwestern University Press, 1966.

FINKLE, JASON L. and GABLE, RICHARD W. (eds.). *Political Development and Social Change.* New York: John Wesley and Sons, Inc., 1966.

FORTES, M. and EVANS-PRITCHARD, E. E. (eds.). *African Political Systems.* London: Oxford University Press, 1940.

GEERTZ, CLIFFORD (ed.). *Old Societies and New States.* New York: The Free Press of Glencoe, 1963.

HALLOWELL, JOHN H. (ed.). *Development: For What?* Durham, N.C.: Duke University Press, 1964.

HEILBRONNER, ROBERT L. *The Great Ascent: The Struggle for Economic Development.* New York: Harper and Row, 1963.

KAUTSKY, JOHN H. (ed.). *Political Change in Underdeveloped Countries.* New York: John Wiley and Sons, 1962.

LEVY, MARION J. *Modernization and The Structure of Societies.* Princeton, N.J.: Princeton University Press, 1966.

LIPSET, S. M. *Political Man.* Garden City, N.Y.: Doubleday and Co., 1960.

LYSTAD, ROBERT A. (ed.). *The African World: A Survey of Social Research.* New York: Frederick A. Praeger, 1965.

MEHDEN, FRED R. VON DER. *Politics of the Developing Nations.* Englewood Cliffs, N.J.: Prentice-Hall, 1964.

MOORE, BARRINGTON. *Political Power and Social Theory.* New York: Harper and Row, 1965.

MYRDAL, GUNNAR. *Economic Theory and Underdeveloped Regions.* London: Gerald Duckworth and Co., Ltd., 1957.

ORGANSKI, A. F. K. *The Stages of Political Development.* New York: Alfred A. Knopf, 1965.

PENNOCK, J. ROLAND (ed.). *Self-Government in Modernizing Nations.* Englewood Cliffs, N.J.: Prentice-Hall, 1964.

PYE, LUCIAN W. *Politics, Personality, and Nation Building.* New Haven, Conn.: Yale University Press, 1962.

———. *Aspects of Political Development.* Boston: Little, Brown and Company, 1966.

ROSTOW, WALT W. *The Stages of Economic Growth.* New York: Cambridge University Press, 1960.

SHILS, EDWARD A. *Political Development in the New States.* The Hague: Mouton and Co., 1965.

WARD, ROBERT E. *Studying Politics Abroad: Field Research in the Developing Areas.* Boston: Little, Brown and Co., 1964.

WALLERSTEIN, IMMANUEL (ed.). *Social Change: The Colonial Situation.* New York: John Wiley and Sons, Inc., 1966.

2 ·

The Impact of the
International System
upon Africa

The traditional, Eurocentric nation-state system has undergone considerable change since its inauguration at Westphalia in 1648. The distinctive nature of the post-World War II system can be understood only in contrast to the traditional system. The foremost characteristic of the traditional system was its hierarchical configuration. That is, a state assumed a role of a great or lesser power according to its capacity to enforce its will upon other powers. The cost of conducting war and the risks entailed were an acceptable part of most attempts to resolve political conflicts.

While it is true that the traditional international system imposed no objective restraints upon national actors, prudent statesmen were always cognizant of the international power relationships. The maintenance of a balance of power lent a tolerable stability to international politics. But, despite the prudent statesman's penchant for stability, the transition from the traditional international system to a new system was almost inevitable; for the old order contained the forces of its own destruction.

As a result of forces precipitated within the traditional international system, Africa and the non-West gained the capacity to influence the dynamics of international politics. This new phenomenon was implicit in the old order; it occurred in spite of, and not because of, the new states of Africa and the non-West. The African states, acquired their independence by default: the "discount" of technology, the courtesy of the bipolar powers, and the benevolence of the Wilsonian creed granted sovereignty at a bargain price. International politics was no longer synonymous with the politics of Europe—a new international system had been born.

Despite its intellectual convenience, the conflict between Marxist and liberal ideologies never did explain adequately the dynamics of the international order. Immediately after the second World War, it did appear that the world was divided into camps of ideological solidarity; this situation, it is now apparent from hindsight, merely reflected the temporary military preponderance of the bipolar powers. The clash of these contending ideologies certainly contributes to world tensions but in itself does not adequately account for the present scope and depth of international discord.

It has only recently been clearly recognized that a fundamental alteration has taken place in the post-war bipolar pattern of international politics since the 1950's. This transformation derives from a fantastic advance in weapons technology, the resulting dangers of nuclear war, and the generally increasing functional interdependence of all states. More relevant to this study is the decrease in usable force and situational capability of the bipolar powers, and the vigorous revival—or initial appearance—of nationalistic sentiments in those states.

In other words, there is a trend towards the diffusion and decentralization of power, new channels of application, and reassigned objectives. The new international environment is characterized by a general increase in the number of politically-active participants. These national actors operate pluralistically across a broad spectrum of political alternatives in a manner which appears to the outside observer to be both unstructured and unsystematic. The trend is in the direction of complex global patterns of shifting and overlapping loyalties and political obligations. National actors often find their interests to be best served by countervailing, rather than unidirectional, actions and obligations.

The new states of Africa and the non-West add new dimensions to the evolving international system. It remains to be determined which of the following questions is more appropriate to a fruitful line of inquiry: Will the new international system adapt itself to African and non-Western forces? Or, will Africa and the non-West, as they seek to join the system, find it necessary to become increasingly Western?

FORCES OF CHANGE
IN THE INTERNATIONAL SYSTEM

The various contemporary revolutions in technology, coupled with the widening horizons of human thought, have undermined the historically accepted political ideas and patterns which have developed since the Renaissance and the Reformation. We live today in a frontierless world, where states, old and new, are simultaneously frustrated and challenged by the expanding agenda of international politics. All seek fresh means of organizational and institutional modernization in order to relate themselves to one another and to the total international environment.

It is interesting to note that a similar breakdown of frontiers occurred in the fifteenth and sixteenth centuries when the Renaissance and Reformation initiated the processes of secularization of Western man's thought and nationalization of his concept of religion. The combined forces of these movements sparked a revolution in the loyalties and allegiances of Western man. The Christian synthesis of the medieval period was ultimately destroyed: from its ruins emerged the nation-state system.

During the heyday of the Eurocentric nation-state system, colonialism was the basis of the relationship between Europe and the non-West. In the seventeenth and eighteenth centuries the possession of colonies served as an outlet for the energies of the European peoples and, in addition, enhanced the prestige of the ruling dynasties. With the transfer of sovereignty from the monarch to the nation during the nineteenth and twentieth centuries, the hopes of such romantics as Mazzini for a harmonious world of coexisting nationalities were dimmed. The desire of the masses for a "place in the sun" seemed to be no less than the desire of the monarchs had been. The populist Primrose League in Britain and Pan-German League in Germany attacked such inward-looking policies as Gladstone's "masterly inactivity" and Bismarck's idea of *Kleindeutschland*.

Strategic considerations further prompted colonial expansion during the latter part of the nineteenth century. Coaling stations and key passageways such as the Suez, Panama, Djibouti, and Vladivostok were acquired by the great powers to insure their world-wide interests.

The productive capacities of the industrial revolution prompted entrepreneurs to seek new markets for mass-produced goods and additional sources of raw materials. And men who were becoming superfluous as means in the production process found an attractive escape in such areas as South Africa and Algeria. A wholly economic interpretation of late nineteenth-century colonial expansion, however, does not pertain to the real world where irrational drives of national pride and messianism play decisive roles.

After 1945, Europeans turned inward, and began rebuilding and revising their economic and social systems. They adopted pragmatic means to insure their material happiness. More sophisticated industries developed atop an infrastructure which had been left essentially intact, despite the destruction of the war; these new industries were oriented for their materials and markets toward Europe. Finally, rather than allowing a segment of the population to remain alienated from the mainstream of the socio-economic system, attempts were made to filter wealth to the bottom level of the social structure.

In the post-1945 period the strategic assumptions which induced the European powers to acquire world-wide empires have been modified: thermonuclear weaponry has altered the demands of strategic advantage. Soviet missiles in Siberia or Cuba are equally capable of levelling Boston. Conventional war is anathema to nuclear powers that fear escalation. Guerrilla wars, which the great powers have shown themselves inept at conducting, have become the most readily available means of conflict resolution. One effect of technology has been, in other words, to give the great powers a handicap in political conflicts.

The authority of the European colonial culture was discredited in the eyes of non-Westerners by the cataclysm of the First World War; the Second World War vitiated European power around the globe. During the Second World War Europe consumed itself. In 1945 there seemed to be nothing left of a civilization which had spawned two flanking giants, the United States and the Soviet Union.

The bipolar powers were a different breed from the traditional great powers of Europe. Their expanse was greater than all of Europe and their power depended on internal development rather than on the conquest of other sovereignties. As international actors, they consolidated their spheres of power. Yet, although the traditional justifications for empire were discredited in the post-1945 period, power invariably seeks to become authoritative.

In assessing their national interests, Russia and the United States discovered that traditional notions of what was "good" for the state were not what they desired. The two states imagined themselves to be the new vehicles of the spirit of the French Revolution. As the Napoleonic armies had toppled the house of cards of the traditional European order, the United States and Russia brought a revolutionary spirit to the rest of the world. In legend, if not in fact, both states were conceived in revolution; both revolutions sought the liberation of the individual from traditional communal forms. They concurred that the traditional bases for order in the non-West—tribalism, kinship, monarchy, and tyranny—were to be replaced by the new orders of either liberal democracy or communism.

The revolution won the mind of the non-West. Western ideas conveyed by Russia and the United States were solvents of authority, be it imposed by the traditional European powers or the new bipolar powers. Concomitants of the pseudo-scientific communistic and liberal ideologies were an attitude of critical doubt and the scientific method. These attitudes gave the non-West a new soul and a new face.

THE IMPACT OF CHANGE
UPON AFRICA

The environmental changes in Africa have outstripped the institutional structures of the tribal era. Such Western concepts as the nation-state, the secular city, economic motivation, and a progressive as opposed to a static vision of reality have invaded the African continent. The promise of higher stages of material and spiritual perfection is competing with the negative condition of primitive African existence.

The stages of development in Africa, however, are not as neatly differentiated as the nineteenth-century evolutionists might have claimed. There is no inner order to the course of history which guarantees the universal pre-eminence of one mode of civilization and the total capitulation of all others. Recent events in Africa might well serve as sufficient evidence to vitiate any formalized image of the process of Westernization. For the impact of the West upon Africa has been a complex process, not to be understood by formulating a monolinear scheme.

Rather, the relationship between West and non-West is to be understood dialectically. Intrinsic to the West was the aspiration to disseminate its way of life among other peoples, to broaden the scope and the horizon of Western civilization. On one hand, the technological, cultural, and economic norms of the West changed the environment of non-Western peoples. On the other hand, the colonial powers preserved their domination without initially realizing that the opening of the non-West, its incorporation into world history, and its creative attitudes would invariably change the face of the West. This interaction is the dialectic of the West and the non-West.

This dialectic has been of greater significance to Europeans than the Copernican revolution in the natural sciences. The European's awareness of alien values and mores seemed to strip traditional verities of their cosmic significance. Not until the twentieth century, however—most decisively since 1945—did the European "exclusive club" concept of the international system become obsolete. The dialectic meant that the West, in fulfilling its universalistic ideals, lost them both as absolutes and as its specific property.

The element of Western culture that is now proving irresistible to African elites is something more fundamental than any technological manifestations: it is the dedication to the use of rational processes and critical doubt which underlie science and technology. This means the willingness and the effort to seek and systematically apply evidence and analysis in many different aspects of life. It implies a receptivity to change regarding one's ideas.

Scientific knowledge is power which can be used to shape the environment and the behavior of men. It has prodded the revolutionary temper of African elites and reinforced the assumption that there is no achievement impossible of attainment through hard work.

The "tyranny of the test tube" has undermined the time-honored bases for accepting propositions as true or as sufficient to warrant action. In African tradition, myth and religion have a far greater hold on many more aspects of life than they do in the West. Children grow to adulthood in a world saturated with non-science—with a deep-running view of nature that is essentially non-rational and non-objective. It is a world in which an epidemic calls for special prayer flags no less than for immunization. But immunization is proving to be more effective than prayer flags. And, just as people in the West have learned to rely on immunization and to leave less to prayer, so in Africa the evidence is bound to shatter traditional beliefs.

African leaders may feel impelled by pride or politics to sing the praises of their peoples' traditions and spiritual excellence. But in their desire for national independence, dignity, and prestige, they find Western industrial, agricultural, and military techniques attractive. The leaders plead for an Africa that is essentially African, yet they are fully aware of the human tragedy of their peoples' scanty production levels and miserable living conditions.

The introduction of new and alien techniques and values into a community ultimately affects its social structure, as well as its economic and political patterns. The community's cultural foundations are threatened, its religion called in question, and its basic philosophies forced to accommodate new pressures and conditions. It is this very revolution in the African outlook on life that is providing the foundation, taking the initial, minute, but measurable steps, toward a "closed" world culture.

If this trend toward the conversion of an African to a Western culture is in fact occurring, what is its impact on the nature and sources of international conflict and co-operation? Perhaps the closing of the gap between cultures will provide a universal criterion for dialogue. Approaches to problems, concepts, and their conclusions will be based on evidence accessible to all, rather than on parochial dogmas, impressions, or emotions. The community of mankind would be strengthened in a world where the spirit of free inquiry faced all forms of tyranny, external and internal.

In such a world, a sense of community might develop and eventually diminish the claims of national sovereignty. A transmutation of human nature and a new and broader spirit of community is necessary to the achievement and endurance of world order. Little is known about the development of such a spirit, but it may be that, just as improved communications and transportation are providing workable physical bases for international community, so may the propagation of a common way of approaching the world and its problems be laying the cultural foundations.

THE EVOLVING INTERNATIONAL SYSTEM

The states of today's world exist and function within a "closed" international system. As man has opened and vastly broadened new areas of human activity and intellectual exploration, the system of international relations has become increasingly compressed. No matter what its geographical relationship to other states in the international system, no rumble of discontent, no major development in the internal affairs of an individual state can pass unnoticed. Today, the effects of a state's internal developments radiate outwards, producing action and inducing reaction among the other states in a manner which affects the entire system. International politics has grown to be an exceedingly intimate affair. One effect of this new intimacy has been to thrust former colonies and former colonial powers together, to bring the established "natives" of the system into sharper confrontation with a substantial number of recently-arrived "intruders" to the system.

The states of today conduct their relations with each other in a manner quite different from that of a century ago. The rigid and hierarchical status system in which states pursued their foreign policies and their conflicts has given way to a more flexible and egalitarian system.

The independence of African and other non-Western states and their entry into the international system resembles the sudden eruption of the bourgeoisie into post-feudal politics. In a similar manner, the new and small states consider the sanctified, aristocratic values of international politics irrelevant to their own concerns and aspirations.

The form and substance of international political life are no longer dictated by Washington, Moscow, Paris, London, or Bonn. Cairo, Accra, Nairobi, and scores of other capitals now figure prominently in the conduct and direction of international political life. At the time of its establishment in 1945, the United Nations had a total membership of 51 states. Two decades later, this number had increased to 126. In 1945, there were only four African states in the United Nations; today there are 41.*

A more critical and significant factor of system turbulence and change is the nature of the newcomers to international political life. More than half of today's actors in the international political system are non-Western newcomers to that system. No longer do white, Christian, Western people provide the only force in international political life; they are today confronted with a new force of steadily increasing size and momentum: the African and other non-Western peoples and civilizations.

The response of the older societies and their leaders to this phenomenon has been one of distress and, not infrequently, resentment. This distress has taken many forms, one of which is implicit in the increased criticism levelled at international organizations in general, and the United Nations in particular. The United Nations has certainly not fulfilled every expectation of those who saw in its establishment the "hope of mankind." It is possible that of the many critics who have labelled it a mere "debating forum," several mean by this only that they are unwilling to accept the drastic shifts in the balance of its membership.

What these critics are actually saying is that they neither like nor approve of the new composition and direction of the United Nations and, furthermore, of the entire international system. These changes in the international system have been accompanied by changes in the nature of international politics as well. Both lesser and great powers have been left with ill-defined roles.

Two primary factors have given international life its peculiar flavor in the post-1945 period. The great powers no longer govern the dynamics of the state system and, as a corollary, the lesser powers enjoy a wider spectrum of political alternatives.

---

*Including the Republic of South Africa. With the recent independence of Swaziland and Equatorial Guinea, the number of independent African states has reached 41.

The great powers lack the situational capability to deal with the course of events in the non-West and Africa. The very fact that they possess thermonuclear weaponry compels them to deploy conventional forces cautiously: the threat of escalation to the nuclear threshold is a constant restraint. A moral stigma has been attached to unilateral interference by the present bipolar powers in the areas of the world formerly dominated by the traditional European powers.

Therefore, the days are past when a great power could intervene anywhere at will to guard its perceived interests. In 1879, Britain and France could assume control of Egyptian finances to insure the payment of debts by the Turkish viceroy; in 1956, they could not militarily prevent the nationalization of the Suez Canal. In the 1890's, Belgium controlled intransigent natives by lopping off their hands; in the Congo crisis of 1960, the involvement of the great powers was restricted to the operational channels provided by an international body.

The most obvious change resulting from these factors was a shift in the locus of great power conflict resolution out of Europe to the African and non-Western world. Until the Second World War, most great power rivalries were settled on the continent of Europe, even when the issues included the status of non-European territories. The Russo-Japanese War of 1904–05 was the first instance in modern history when a major war occurred outside the continent; the Japanese-American conflict of 1941–45 was the second. When wars did occur outside of Europe, they were usually extensions of a conflict among European powers. The War of the Austrian Succession (1740–48) and the Seven Years' War (1756–63) are classic examples of Anglo-French conflict carried over into the colonial areas of the world.

Since World War II, however, the stabilization of Europe, the disintegration of empires, and revolutionary movements in the non-West have shifted the locus of great power conflict resolution outside of Europe. The French fought the Indo-Chinese and Algerian wars against the externally supported nationalists; the French and British engaged the Egyptians at Suez in 1956. The Americans could not avoid involvement in the Congo and Vietnam.

Of equal significance are the reversed trends in warfare. Were it not for the emergence of African and non-Western states, the chances are that the utility of conventional warfare would have diminished more than it has. In the West, the mutual possession of weapons of total destruction and invulnerable delivery systems has established a stalemate in which antagonists tend to avoid armed clashes of any sort, nuclear or non-nuclear. The viability of Western states precludes insurgencies; the antagoists therefore cannot engage in unconventional warfare in the Western world by encouraging and supporting armed dissidents.

The situation is entirely different, however, in the non-West. In the first place, non-Western states do not possess a nuclear delivery capability; the restraints imposed by the bipolar strategic balance do not exist. War between non-Western states, therefore, remains a realistic probability. Secondly, most non-Western countries have non-viable political systems, which means there are often good prospects for successful insurgent wars. Hence, governments in the non-West pursue their objectives through unconventional warfare.

It may be said, then, that the human being as a weapons system has been given a lease on life with the emergence of the non-West. Combat soldiers retain their importance. Quantitative relations among enemies are still significant. The French lost in Indo-China and Algeria because, among other things, conscription restrictions and economic factors prohibited the fielding of a sufficiently large force. Territory again becomes significant. Buffer states can still serve classical purposes.

Only through such unobtrusive techniques as aid can the great powers attempt to influence the course of African events. The fact that both great powers are forced to rely on alms-giving as a medium of political pressure demonstrates their impotence on the African continent.

The emergence of Africa seems, though perhaps only for the short run, to be enlightening and humanizing the manner in which the wealthier states interpret their interests. "The national interest" is a common justification for contemporary aid programs. Aid is intended, for example, to protect investments, stimulate the donor's economy, promote world stability, develop export markets, achieve influence, or prevent the influence of hostile powers. Thus, co-operative undertakings with little hope of quick political or economic reward are, for the present, a new and important element in international relations. This co-operation has assumed the most hopeful form in the multilateral arrangements for giving. Many states are becoming accustomed to surrendering a measurable—if small—part of their wealth and skills to agencies which they do not fully control and for purposes which, at best, contribute only to their long-range national values.

The broad range of political choice open to the lesser African states and their jealous maintenance of sovereign prerogatives have burst the geographical parameters and vitiated the consensual basis of the traditional state system. Nonetheless, these states have fallen into step with the assumptions of the traditional international system of a political world of sovereign states. All attempts to bring a united Africa to the international political stage have failed; African elites have discovered that racial, historical, and religious bonds are operationally severed by political boundaries—boundaries which were in fact artificially imposed upon their continent by the European powers.

The fact that many African states, successors to colonial territories, are economic and political absurdities merely exacerbates the intensity of African nationalism. It is probably good that intercontinental conflicts of interest, those hardy concomitants of political sovereignty and nationalism, diffuse hostility. Otherwise, a cataclysmic war of the races, or at least international tension on a massive scale, could conceivably be a long-range result of the entry of the non-West into the international system. Were it not for the will and ability of the African states to preserve their sovereignties, the participation of Africa in the international system would be a source of far graver conflict among the great powers than it is now.

Of course, the African states are not the political equals of the bipolar powers in international politics. They are not factors to be reckoned with in the global balance of power. But the fact remains that Morocco can actively work for the elimination of Mauritania, and Somalia can attempt to annex territory on its northern, western, and southern borders. In the modern, compressed state system such policies may have far-reaching consequences.

Painfully aware of their actual weaknesses, however, the overriding assumption of African leaders of whatever political persuasion is to preserve themselves from foreign encroachment. African states have not concentrated around any one power center. They have, in general, a desire not to become dependent on any single country for economic aid or for protection of their domestic power. They have no tradition of democratic centralism and no ideal of subservience to a single dogma with a single infallible interpretation.

Insofar as they succeed in preserving their autonomy, the African states obviate the need for the United States, for example, to become unduly alarmed over the machinations of the Soviet Union. The alleged tendencies of the African intellectuals toward socialism and toward anti-colonialism cannot be equated with tendencies toward subservience to the Soviet Union, or China, or toward acceptance of any state's lead in foreign policy.

The attitude of the African leaders toward the great power rivalry is illustrated by the fact that Soviet and Chinese aid programs have not substantially altered the domestic or foreign policies of the African states. Many of the African states aided by the Soviets and Chinese are accepting aid from Western countries as well. The African statesmen who pass through Moscow, Peking, and Washington make no secret of their intention to exploit both the Eastern and Western powers for economic aid without relinquishing any political autonomy.

The communist countries furnished weapons and funds to Algerian nationalists during the rebellion against French rule. But the nationalists, once in power, outlawed the Algerian Communist Party. For aid, they continue to rely primarily on France, who is in the best position to provide that aid. China, at great cost to herself, has given grants to Egypt and other African states. Yet, Egypt responded to the Sino-Indian border war by offering small arms to Nehru. Morocco, too, has benefited from communist aid. Yet, she banned participation by the Communist party in the referendum campaign on King Hassan's draft constitution. The popular American impression that wily communist aid programs somehow make vast inroads on unsuspecting African states is unfounded.

Africa is less and less the plaything of the Great Powers. Africans often express the fear, or perhaps conviction, that they are pawns in the cold war. But it might be argued reasonably that the United States, the Soviet Union, China, and the other great powers have become the pawns of the Africans. Hence, the power of the non-powers has indeed brought to the fore the issue of the "tyranny of the weak" in present-day international politics.

BIBLIOGRAPHY

DEAN, VERA M. *The Nature of the Non-Western World.* New York: Mentor Books, 1957.

EMERSON, RUPERT. *From Empire to Nation.* Cambridge, Mass.: Harvard University Press, 1960.

GOULD, PETER R. (ed.). *Africa: Continent of Change.* Belmont, Calif.: Wadsworth Publishing Co., 1961.

JACKSON, BARBARA WARD. *The Interplay of East and West.* New York: W. W. Norton and Co., 1957.

————. *Five Ideas that Changed the World.* New York: W. W. Norton and Co. 1959.

————. *The Rich Nations and the Poor Nations.* New York: W. W. Norton and Co., 1962.

LANGER, WILLIAM. *The Diplomacy of Imperialism.* New York: Alfred A. Knopf, 1935.

LENSEN, GEORGE A. *The World Beyond Europe.* Boston: Houghton Mifflin Co., 1960.

MOON, P. T. *Imperialism and World Politics.* New York: The Macmillan Co., 1926.

NORTHROP, FILMER S. C. *The Meeting of East and West.* New York: The Macmillan Co., 1946.

TOYNBEE, ARNOLD. *The World and the West.* New York: Oxford University Press, 1953.

3 ·

Problems of Continuity and Change

The various African states are experiencing difficulties in finding themselves and determining the crucial questions of their national destinies. The introduction of Western techniques and the emergence of a scientific spirit of critical doubt in limited areas of life will lead to ever wider changes in the culture of African states, just as it has in the West. Political, social, and economic development are all closely intertwined. Interference in one area necessitates adjustment in the others.

The Western values grafted hastily onto African states have yet to take: the new notions and systems of thought have yet to be assimilated into a meaningful framework. The alien-inspired sense of direction is searching for a native sense of proportion—a drive toward some substantive goal of high achievement.

The collision of venerated tribal values, Islamic traditions, Western concepts, and the realities of the present international environment underlie the existential problem of Africa. The principal crisis facing the new states is one of coexistence with each other and acclimation to their new political milieu. The

African present is suspended between two developmental phases: a past of tribalism, struggling against extinction; and a future of nationhood, fighting for survival. In order to save its life, the continent faces the danger of losing its soul.

During recent years, nearly the whole continent has gained independence from foreign domination. Unfortunately, however, liberation has been achieved at a time of crisis for the traditional territorial state. The Africans' lack of economic self-sufficiency leaves them unable to enjoy their new status of self-responsibility. Political developments in Africa have outrun cultural development, and African self-consciousness has not caught up with the existential predicament.

The new states are now only just beginning to realize that their new status as independent entities carries with it an awesome collection of problems and responsibilities. Independence constitutes only a thin shell into which the essence and content of true statehood must be poured; and many of the new states are being forced to acknowledge their inability to fill this shell.

THE TRIBAL BASE

In many cases, the most important hindrance to political stability in the African states is the lingering reality of tribalism. This has been true particularly in the sub-Saharan states. Yet not all aspects of tribalism have proven detrimental to African statehood. The tribe can be an effective unit of support for leaders and a rallying point for nationalism.

The desire for individual freedom seems to be a relatively insignificant force in the African states. Indeed, the ordinary African has experienced very little freedom at any time in history, and there is no cultural heritage to evoke such a desire. Under ancient tribal organization, individual liberty was as rare as it was under colonial domination. The centuries-long traditions and beliefs inherent to tribal societies remain deeply ingrained in the lives of most Africans.

The traditional unit of society was the tribe. Its real rulers were not kings or emperors, but family patriarchs, councils of elders, village chiefs, and clan heads. Such men represented the only sources of political authority. A tribal state was formed when a village chieftain or warrior clan extended control over a large number of uncentralized villages and thus formed a kingdom. It was possible for such authority to be superimposed upon the existing societal structures without impairing the functions of either the village organization or the state.

Each group in the tribal state had a status according to lineage and a role commensurate with its occupation. When the state expanded, some type of territorial arrangement became operative as the chief appointed representatives in each of the areas under his control. These "governors" provided the ritual link with the king and performed political functions, such as collection of taxes and tributes and conscription of armies.

The tribal state, it must be emphasized, was not based on political or territorial sovereignty or unity. Rather, it embraced a diversity of groups, all at different stages of development, and each with its own set of beliefs and ways of life. These groups became parts of a diffuse sphere of influence which was defined by social strata rather than by territorial boundaries. The king or emperor was not desirous of territory for its own sake. Instead, he sought to form and maintain functional relationships with groups which could provide arms, men, money, and goods. In return, he served as their spiritual authority and protector from alien tribes in times of war.

Under the umbrella of the imperial protectorate, each unit maintained its own religious, social, and political organizations; these were left virtually untouched by the political superstructure of the tribal empire. Consequently, the empire or state was merely an aggregation of kin groupings which had little in common other than a mystical relationship with some distant protective suzerain. It could scarcely even be called a "geographical expression."

THE RELIGIOUS BASE

Since the rise of Islam in the early seventh century, Muslims have carried their banners into Africa through conquest, slavery, trade, and missionary education. Today Muslims constitute the largest single religious group in the African continent; of three hundred million Africans, there are approximately one hundred million Muslims, forty million Christians and one hundred sixty million members of various animistic pagan sects. Islamic peoples occupy more than half of the almost twelve million square miles of the African area. Of the 41 independent African states, 15 are exclusively or predominantly Islamic, and in 7 other states, the Muslims constitute the largest single religious community.

The proportion of African Muslims is greater today than at any time in the entire history of the African continent, and the number is expected to rise. During the last thirty years alone, the number of Muslims has more than doubled from forty million. The historic Christian-animistic barrier, which stretched from Senegal across old French Africa and the Southern Sudan to Ethiopia, Uganda, and Tanganyika has collapsed.

But in spite of its undeniable ubiquity, the relationship between Islamic presence and influence in Africa is, at best, paradoxical. It would be folly to speak of an African Islamic homogeneous whole. Muslim Africa is a varied assortment of peoples, a mosaic of schisms, and a diversity of political loyalties.

Arising from a seventh-century social protest movement in Arabia, the ethical system of prophet Muhammad was essentially a vigorous reaffirmation of ideas common to most monotheistic doctrines. Among these, the prophet emphasized that all members of the new Islamic community were brothers of equal individual intrinsic worth: differences arise between men only in terms of their status, wealth, ability, and the relationships that these factors create. All members of the Islamic community are joined together by common loyalties and outward and inward obligations to the one God. Muhammad also included basic ethical guidelines governing conduct towards non-Muslims who accepted political control of the Islamic community: toleration of diverse beliefs was generally dependent on payment of a tributary tax, but non-believers, though allowed to participate in commercial and social life, were never to be granted full brotherhood with the Muslims.

Early Islam was oriented in a specific direction as revealed by the Koran and the teachings of the Prophet. Doctrinal differences and varying interpretations of the Koranic revelations were so slight that a purity of belief and cohesiveness was possible. Early religious leaders met the challenges of varying interpretations not by asserting what was to be accepted but by stating that the divergent views were unacceptable. This early laxity paved the way for a flexibility of interpretation that would allow later Muslims to adapt Islamic teachings to the conditions of their particular areas, synthesizing it with local beliefs and cultures in order to meet local needs. Yet, they remained basically Islamic. In this way, the widest possible moral unity was maintained in the community.

In the later evolution of Islamic doctrine, the Koran was accepted as absolute, and the ethical content of Islamic law was interpreted to fit the needs of society. Recognizing that purely local interpretations presented a danger of community disintegration, early religious leaders developed a body of traditions based on decisions which the Prophet had made in specific cases. These traditions served as guidelines for jurists and scholars in applying the Koran to their specific circumstances. Thus, Islam was able to resist collapse, in spite of the lack of any centralized clergy or church hierarchy. By its flexibility and adaptiveness, Islamic culture was able to withstand an influx of new peoples, ideas, traditions, political pressures, and military invasions.

The Muslims exposed large areas of Africa to a civilization based on a monotheistic religion. Islam, and later, Christianity, superimposed a faith in a supreme controlling force in the personality of an omnipotent God upon ancient animistic beliefs. Yet, the legacy of animism persisted. Where Islam and Christianity ran counter to these beliefs, they were practically destroyed. But non-conflicting or complementary beliefs were able to coexist and even to strengthen one another. Religious dualism became widespread as parallel practices were accepted into the tribal ritual and doctrine.

Islamic ritual, for example, was linked to neither clergy nor an organized church and consequently was adaptable to many tribal societies. The emphasis on magic and other forms of spiritualism, as well as the wide variations in belief and in practice characteristic of Islam, reduced the strain between the African and the Islamic community.

Islam also facilitated the introduction of new elements of material culture, most importantly, a written language. These new stimuli made possible the rise of new commercial and administrative classes to administer the tribal state's business and manage its public affairs. New classes took their place alongside the myriad of religious groupings within the same political units.

One of the most important effects of the spread of Islam was its usefulness as an instrument of authority. Islam conceives of man as a creation of and for the service of God. In subsequent practice and interpretation, this implies that social welfare is not a proper concern of government. The Islamic political heritage engendered a widespread disinclination to work with or through a government to bring education and prosperity to the people. Over the centuries there developed a basic indifference to the legitimacy of government. There is little operational distinction between *de jure* and *de facto* government in Islamic political practice.

Islamic political traditions have bred attitudes of submissiveness in areas which have had close contact with Muslim beliefs and doctrines. It is precisely these attitudes of deference that modern Islamic leaders are able to utilize in establishing and consolidating positions of personal power.

Although many Islamic institutions and rituals were incorporated into tribal societies, the basic universalist tenets of Islam were unacceptable to African traditionalists. Islam thus became one of many elements in African culture, adding knowledge through its universities and schools, but remaining divorced from effective control of society.

African Islam has produced a fragile political synthesis, and the Islamization of Africa remains superficial. The schismatic Muslim priests *(marabouts)* and the many religious fraternities *(sufi tariqahs)* profess a more mystical and intuitive kind of religion than scholastic Islam, and one often associated with the worship of local saints and other local superstitions and customs. In addition, the Maliki doctrine, the Islamic interpretation in most of Africa, through its emphasis on consensus *(ijma)* as a source of law, encouraged deviation from orthodoxy.

Though Islam, mainly through Arab influence, has registered spectacular numerical gains during the last few decades, there is no homogeneous society of African Muslims. Islamic unity in Africa remains an aspiration rather than a political reality. The common denominator of Negro Islam lies in its very heterogeneity: nothing unites the Muslims of Nigeria with those of Somalia.

The process of assimilation of Christianity into tribal life has followed a similar course. Through the efforts of European missionaries and colonial regimes, Africans were introduced to Christian beliefs and practices. While it is true that there were many converts, these were primarily among Westernized elites who adopted Christian teachings only in part, just as they adopted selected Western philosophical values.

So far, Christianity as a religion has made little impact on the life of the African masses. Like Islam, in many areas it lives side by side with traditional animistic beliefs and practices. Its greatest impact has not been through outright conversion to Christian beliefs and practices, but through the introduction of Western culture and values as taught in the mission schools.

Just as Islam's greatest impact has been through the introduction of new techniques of learning, Christianity's has been through the education of Africans in new modes of thought and work. Most of what Africa has learned from Christian missions is essentially secular. The Christian values which Africans consider desirable are closely identified with modern, wealthy states of the West. Most African Christians are less interested in Christianity's intrinsic meaning than they are in its value as a symbol of progress, wealth, and social well-being.

THE COLONIAL LEGACY

While Africans are grateful to Western Europe for a great deal, they are quite justified in their condemnation of colonialism. The bright light of colonialism also cast a dark shadow.

The colonial period was one of cultural dislocation and, above all, lack of purpose. The colonial sources of power and decision had no relevance to the African heritage. Upon achieving independence, Africa was left with two stark choices: either renounce the relevance of its tradition to its present aspirations, or baptize change within the spirit of that tradition. The first was both impossible to achieve and dangerous for the infant African states to attempt. Hence, it became imperative for the new African states to develop a unique sense of purpose in order to provide the framework within which to interpret their own aspirations. In this they have not wholly succeeded.

It is more meaningful for the new African states to interpret this sense of purpose in terms of national progress than as an attempt to "catch up" with the West. Progress, measured on a uniquely African scale, is the only meaningful term which can guide Africa's fight for development. It is not to be sought on traditional African standards alone, nor solely on Western or European standards. Progress must be *all* that is adaptable and necessary for the realization of the full stature of independence and growth of the African personality.

There is by no means agreement among African states on the specific details of this objective, that is, the form and content of progress, or the political and economic philosophies to be applied in order to achieve it. There is, however, consensus on the basic premise that progress can be achieved by a broad adaptation and integration of global ideas, ideals, and techniques within a distinct intellectual and political atmosphere.

Europe, and with it Western Christianity, brought to Africa new political, economic, and social goals. But in doing so, it disrupted established tribal institutions and partially shattered a way of life. To understand the extent of colonialism's impact, it is necessary to examine its varieties in more detail.

European Colonial Philosophies

The British, although somewhat coy about home rule for the African colonies in the early days of domination, based their colonial policies on the assumption of eventual independence. Britain believed that its civilization could be grafted onto African political, social, and economic structures without any elaborate program of conscious assimilation. It was felt that through British example, and through acquaintance with British practices and values, Africa would automatically accept British civilization. Thus, Britain was concerned with developing loyal native bureaucracy, but not with creating a new African who was merely the local version of a Briton. Britain's was more a policy of guidance and training than of conscious assimilation and Europeanization.

Primarily because of the paucity of British land forces in Africa and the need to control vast areas of territory, Britain ruled its colonies indirectly through the "dual mandate" system. Britain refrained from disrupting African tribal society and relied on the authority of the local chiefs. The British did not believe in overall standardization, as did the French; consequently, Africans were not given a thoroughly British education or British-style government designed to make the African colonies an extension of the metropolitan power.

Britain was mainly concerned with making certain that it would lose as little money as possible through its connections with the colonies: Africa was not to be a burden on the home economy or government. One way to assure this was to avoid a large overseas staff by training Africans to conduct their own affairs. Britain would provide general guidance and liberal amounts of aid, but it would not compromise its own position through an over-extension of its resources.

Britain wanted to make its colonies as self-sufficient as possible but, at the same time, to maintain close political and economic ties. The British government saw an advantage in having readily available resources in order to protect worldwide interests. Britain sought to provide the colonies with a degree of training and self-sufficiency which would relieve the burdens of imperial power.

Belgian colonialism was postulated upon the assumption that the advancement of primitive peoples was possible only through a patient striving to develop native civilization according to its own customs, traditions, and language. It did not attempt to Europeanize natives, but it sought rather to equip them for life with greater skills and knowledge suitable to their mentality and environment.

Belgium views its African territories as possessions and not as parts of the metropolitan state. It had neither the French objective of assimilation, nor the British plan for future independence. The Belgian purpose was to develop an African culture that would be literate and informed so that it could meet, without disruption, the contagious influence of Western values.

The Portuguese colonial office regards its African colonies as natural resources. Its colonial possessions are exploited impersonally and brutally. At the core of Portuguese policy lies a paternalism resting on a firm belief that the infantile capacities of the Negro made civilizing him extremely difficult. The ultimate goal of Portuguese policy is assimilation through Europeanization; and assimilation implies miscegenation, a practice which Portuguese administrators have attempted to endow with moral dignity and egalitarian significance.

Assimilation has been the traditional colonial doctrine of the French as well. Though variously interpreted, it essentially meant that the colony was to become an integral part of the mother country, with its society restructured in the French image. Assimilation was a policy of educating natives to think and speak like Frenchmen. Not only did it appeal to the French belief in man's equality and the ever-present desire to disseminate French culture; it also provided the means of unifying colonial administration. Assimilation is a natural part of French thought, thoroughly enveloped in the *mission civilisatrice.*

However, scientific attitudes of the late nineteenth century altered the assimilationist colonial theory. In place of the humanitarian notion of basic equality of all peoples, colonial theorists adopted the neo-Darwinian belief that certain important inequalities exist among races. Natural selection, so interpreted, implied forward movement and social advancement. Affected by these thoughts, French theorists soon denied the possibility of assimilation and insisted on a policy which would preserve racial differences.

With the decline of the doctrine of assimilation, the nation's civilizing mission changed to conform to the ideas expressed by contemporary sociologists. Although the political thinkers of the day felt they were developing a new theory, the result was not a total rejection of assimilation, but a modification of it, called the policy of association.

The great virtue of the association policy was its simplicity, flexibility, and practicality. The need for variation in colonial practice was emphasized. One of its essential tenets was that the determining factors in all colonial policies should be the geographic, ethnic, and social characteristics of the region under French control. Evolution of native groups along their own lines was encouraged. Underlying this notion was the realization that strong co-operation between the colonial and the native was imperative, and it was assumed that this would be best achieved through the retention of native institutions. All subsequent French efforts were directed toward differential regional development; in this task the French and the natives were "associated," each doing what best suited his abilities. This, of course, required a certain degree of local autonomy.

The policy of association was rooted in the belief that economic betterment of a region was to be undertaken by natives and Frenchmen within a general framework of mutual interest and a sort of "fraternity but not equality." Association involved an implicit contractual agreement which envisaged co-operation and coexistence of two different societies placed in artificial contact.

The Alienated Elites

European colonialism produced cultural misfits, men without roots or genuine values. It succeeded only in divorcing the elites from contact with their compatriots; as a result, the elites could find identity only either in the traditional culture that the colonialists had disparaged and repressed, or in total acceptance of foreign values.

Today's African elites are burdened by a conflict of values in their search for identity. One of the most pressing political problems in African states is the establishment of mass support for the leadership groups. Mobilization of the various segments of the population around a systematic framework of national interests is difficult for two reasons: one, a national interest requires commonly held notions of the public good, and such notions have not been crystallized beyond the immediate goal of anti-colonialism; and, two, there are no established means by which a public consensus can be reached by all segments of society.

Colonialism has left behind it a complex legacy of inadequacy; to generate a new and genuine sense of identity, the elite group must struggle to transform a negative revolt into a positive affirmation of the self. Many African leaders are victims of an upbringing which makes them only superficially modern and only superficially African. The West has implanted within them the notion of utilitarianism, but not the essential spiritual values which have made utilitarian success possible. As a result, they tend to confuse means and ends, and to see their culture in its uncreative, ossified, passive side—the side which allowed Africa to be dominated for so long.

The task of leadership of the African elites has cast them as the vehicles of progress and modernization. The operational requirements of leadership have included setting up governments, establishing foreign relationships, and implementing policies.

At present, the problems facing African leaders arise less from external sources than from basic inadequacies of image and perception. African leaders fail to understand or accept either the requirements or the implications of leadership.

There is hardly an African state where leader and follower are in agreement over a well-defined common goal. They lack an appreciation of the major environmental factors they face, especially the definition of the problem to which they see themselves responding. There is little or no consensus upon the major elements of an action program. In other words, the problem of who leads and who follows in Africa is directly related to the disagreement on where to go. The frameworks of national mission erected by African national leaders in the pre-independence era have outgrown their usefulness. The authoritarianism of present African leaders may produce surface acquiescence and even some grudging harmonization of policy, but to coerce perpetually one's people is not to lead them.

During the struggle for independence and the early period of statehood, African leaders effectively satisfied the requirements of leadership. Both targets and programs were clear; with the problem and the mission so sharply defined, issues of leadership were easily and quietly settled. The leaders were extended support by virtual acclamation; in the early days the euphoria of co-operation in the face of foreign domination militated against in-group quarrels.

With the passage of time, however, many African leaders have fallen into the habit of using their people as instruments of their personal power. The dominance of the leaders has fallen under attack and internal struggles for power have ensued.

The crisis of leadership in Africa was inevitable. To a considerable extent the contemporary distemper of leadership in Africa only reflects the success of the original enterprise—the goal to which they committed themselves during the struggle for liberation has been reached. Thus, the African leaders are reaping some unhappy consequences of their own success. Long justifying their own stewardship on the grounds of the magnitude of the threat of foreign domination, these leaders today find themselves with little to offer their people but slogans. The seat of leadership has grown less and less comfortable as economic and political frustrations mount, and as one coup d'état has succeeded another in various African states.

Perhaps inevitably, a perplexing ambivalence now complicates the leader-follower relationship in many African states. On one hand, leaders continue to argue that the imminent threat of foreign domination remains as pernicious as ever. From this postulate flows the chorus of ringing appeals for more sacrifices that constitutes such a great part of the African leaders' rhetoric. On the other hand, however, one finds African leaders transcending their own argument by discovering a new approach to the wealthy capitals in a climate of co-operative endeavours. It is doubtful whether the African leaders today take seriously the dangers from without; they invoke the psychology of crisis only as a method of perpetuating their outworn hegemony. African leadership is a technique limited in its scope and effect to a situation of crisis or tension; it considers leadership and domination synonymous.

The challenge to African leadership is one of combining the massive enterprise of nation-building with a more flexible and many-sided approach on a number of fronts. Such a new attack demands that African leaders face some uncomfortable facts and make some hard decisions. They must seriously attempt to balance the rewards of leadership against its costs. They must realize that the added vitality of a national community outweighs the loss of a leader's freedom of choice and action that a close relationship entails. Otherwise, Africa will be at the mercy of military elites for many years.

Since their independence, the army has served diverse functions within the African states. It has been a symbol of national independence and unity and a sword to guarantee newly won independence from external intervention and tentative unity from internal factionalism. In recent years, through military coups d'état, the army has been escalated to become the most important wielder of political power and influence within fully half of the African states.

A general explanation of the political role assumed by military elites is the crisis of African leadership. The army has assumed significance because of the political default of civilian elites. Many civilian elites who had been the midwives of independence by pamphleteering, agitation, and guerrilla activities proved themselves incapable of delivering the goods for nation-building. After assuming political office, they preferred facile ideological speculation to the wise allocation of social values, reconciliation of conflicting interests, and performance of efficient administration.

Therefore, it is not difficult to understand why the military elites stepped in to fill this political vacuum. They had been trained to implement orders rather than to merely formulate grandiose goals, were desirous of beginning the arduous task of nation-building, intolerant of domestic factionalism, and most importantly, possessed the means of enforcing their will. Outright coups eliminated Ghana's Kwame Nkrumah and Algeria's Ahmed Ben Bella, two of Africa's most vociferous leaders. Even such broadly based civilian parties as Ghana's Convention Peoples' Party (CPP) and Algeria's National Liberation Front (FLN) were incapable of saving these leaders. Other African armies have succeeded in a number of "juggling acts" rather than true coups d'état and assumption of power.

In justifying their assumption of political power, military elites have often stated that they are serving—in interim—the functions normally maintained in the West by the constitutional processes. Nonetheless, such apologies do not fulfill the political necessity of legitimization for the government. Since it is rare that military elites relinquish power to the civilians, they must confront the reality that a state cannot be governed effectively by force. Military elites—like their civilian predecessors—must justify their rule by appealing to the various "isms" in vogue in Africa. Nonetheless, such incantations without delivery of the goods of modernization cannot transform power into legitimacy. Since military governments need both elusive ideological justification and hardly won support, both of which they rarely receive, legitimacy and nation-building are beyond their power. The game of political manipulation and subsequent military coups d'état continue in many African states. It is difficult to assess when and how this game will end.

THE SEARCH FOR NEW VALUES

The tension between Western and African values is disrupting societies at precisely the time when cohesion is the basic prerequisite for progress and modernization. Soon after independence was achieved, African leaders realized the impossibility of imposing alien ideas and ideals on a traditional cultural base. Yet, they also realized that traditional methods and values do not meet the requirements of nationhood in a modern world.

There are at least two essential factors for the successful functioning of any democracy: mass participation and a high degree of political consensus. While the colonial powers could encourage mass participation in government, they failed to initiate a realistic process of social integration to develop political consensus. Western political ideas, with which the new African leaders are so conversant, never had the chance to be implemented in practice. As far as the new Africa is concerned, such ideas shifted into the realm of *ideals*, instead of realistic possibilities for an independent African state.

The impact of the West created a vacuum, not only in the institutional structures of the new African societies, but also in the political thought of the new leaders. This vacuum left only nationalism. It can be filled only after the principles with which the African can completely identify himself have been formulated —and, let it be emphasized, formulated by himself. Only after this process of identification is completed can new institutions which are distinctly African emerge.

The new African is the victim, caught between the "ideals" of the West and the "realities" of his own societies. He is not at home in the West, or the East, or even strange as it may seem, in Africa. He must build, through a process of integration, redefinition, and development of purpose, a new conceptual framework with which to view the rest of the world and himself as a part of it.

In order for the Africans to keep pace with their aspirations, they must translate these aspirations into relevant terms of economic and social reconstruction. Until there is some significant economic and social development, the prospects for the growth of stable political institutions will be dim indeed. The paradox is that without such stable institutions, social and economic development will be retarded.

The African states are finding it difficult to decide on the specific approach which will maximize progress on African terms. Until recently, it was felt that Western political ideas might be completely applicable to African circumstances. But while they provided the framework for the achievement of political independence, the ideals of today's rhetoric are premature and inapplicable to the present realities of African existence.

The agreed-upon objective of the African states is the attainment of modern nationhood. The method to be used, however, remains a subject for widely divergent opinions. The choice seems to lie in a grey zone between the capitalist and the socialist approach.

President Nyerere of Tanzania puts it this way:

> . . . To my mind capitalism went wrong when it divorced wealth from its true purpose. The true purpose of wealth is to satisfy very simple needs; the need for food, the need for shelter, the need for education . . . And socialist countries, no less than capitalist countries, are prepared to behave like the millionaire; and it need not necessarily be a capitalist millionaire—it is just as likely to be a socialist millionaire . . .[1]

Implicit in the above quotation is the representative African attitude toward both capitalism and Soviet socialism, and the desire to offer a corrective to those systems. This same theme, in general, is also expounded by President Senghor of Senegal, who, when writing on African socialism, said:

> We are no 'Marxists' . . . We are socialists. In other words, we shall exclude neither Marx nor Engels from our sources; we shall start from their works as from those of the 'utopian socialists,' and we shall add to these sources the works of their successors and commentators . . . We stand for a middle course, for a democratic socialism which goes so far as to integrate spiritual values, a socialism which ties in with the old ethical current of the French socialists.[2]

On his return from the Soviet Union, former nationalist leader of Senegal Mamadou Dia said, "The Soviet Union has succeeded in building socialism, but at the sacrifice of religion, of the soul."[3]

The new mind of Africa is neither at home in the crucible of Western intellectual, social, and institutional values, nor comfortable with Soviet Communism and the deviations of Marxism. "*Quo Vadis?*"—where are the new states drifting? President Senghor seeks the answer in *negritude* and President Nyerere in African socialism. Most agree that some African form of socialism is the only meaningful method by which progress can be achieved. The question here is not whether socialism is better or worse than any other system. The point of emphasis is the overwhelming desire to create the new—to establish that which is distinctively African.

Within the context of this drift the African states are trying to sustain a sense of direction that will lead them toward positive achievements. The face of Africa reflects uncertainty as well as determination, expediency as well as foresight. Yet this is to be expected, for just as there is a crisis in the relations between the West and Africa, an even greater crisis exists within the soul of Africa.

NOTES

1. Paul E. Sigmund, Jr. *The Ideologies of Developing Nations* (New York: Frederick A. Praeger, 1963), pp. 206-207.

2. *Ibid.*, pp. 207-208 and 244-250.

3. *Ibid.*, p. 244.

BIBLIOGRAPHY

BETTS, RAYMOND F. *Assimilation and Association in French Colonial Theory*, 1890-1914. New York: Columbia University Press, 1961.

DUFFY, JAMES. *Portugal In Africa.* Cambridge, Mass.: Harvard University Press, 1962.

GROVES, CHARLES P. *The Planting of Christianity in Africa.* Vol. III, London: Lutterworth Press, 1964.

HAILEY, WILLIAM M. H. *An African Survey.* (rev. ed.), London: Oxford University Press, 1957.

HENNESSY, MAURICE N. *The Congo: A Brief History and Appraisal.* New York: Frederick A. Praeger, 1961.

HODGKIN, THOMAS and SCHACTER, RUTH. *French-Speaking West Africa in Transition.* New York: Carnegie Endowment for International Peace, 1960.

INGHAM, KENNETH. *A History of East Africa.* New York: Frederick A. Praeger Press, 1962.

LUGARD, FREDERICK C. *The Dual Mandate in British Tropical Africa.* (5th ed.) Hamden, Conn.: Archor Books, 1965.

OLIVER, ROLAND A. and FAGE, J. D. *A Short History of Africa.* Baltimore, Md.: Penguin Books, 1962.

PERHAM, MARGERY F. *Colonial Reckoning.* New York: Alfred A. Knopf, 1962.

SIGMUND, PAUL E. *The Ideologies of the Developing Nations.* New York: Frederick A. Praeger, 1963.

TRIMINGHAM, JOHN SPENCER. *Islam in West Africa.* Oxford: Clarendon Press, 1959.

————. *Islam in East Africa.* Oxford: Clarendon Press, 1964.

WIEDNER, DAVID L. *A History of Africa South of the Sahara.* New York: Random House, 1962.

WIESCHOFF, H. A. *Colonial Policies in Africa.* Philadelphia: University of Pennsylvania Press, 1944.

4 ·

Contemporary African Revolutionary Thought

The title of this chapter is intended to have a dual connotation. It is meant to suggest that a body of peculiarly African revolutionary thought actually exists; but, at the same time, it raises the question whether the postulates and underlying assumptions of contemporary African political thought are truly revolutionary. A view of the numerous varieties of distinguishable forms of African political thought does reveal an apparently revolutionary temper. This is particularly noticeable in African attitudes toward political change and adjustment, the African philosophy of history, and the African image of man.

AFRICAN AMBIVALENCE

At the heart of the African revolutionary temper lies the problem of direction in African history and the concept of a uniquely African personality. The present dialogue expresses the troubled psychological ambivalence of the new Africa: a pattern of attraction to and repulsion from reason, on one hand; and of attraction to and repulsion from submission, on the other. It connects the rational with the irrational and joins objective circumstances with the consciousness of new Africans. It searches for ideal and spiritual elements and beliefs of African character and origin.

The achievement of independence was followed by a period of general disillusionment with the rational idealism of the various African liberation movements. Africa's lack of preparedness combined with this disillusionment to hinder the development of consensus within the ranks of the leaders of the various new states. The absence of consensus has thrown the leaders of newly independent states into confusion as they struggle with ubiquitous social, economic, and political problems. Almost the entire continent has been beset by a reactionary escapism; but, the more moderate African leaders are trying desperately to come to a sober and more sophisticated assessment of their political problems.

The African intelligentsia is confronted by divergent streams of social thought ranging from totalitarianism to a liberalism which includes elements of welfare capitalism and Utopian socialism. Thus, the intelligentsia faces a dilemma. While Africa claims to be moving within a great historical current, rejecting the colonial heritage with its consistent betrayal of democracy to special interests, most of the continent is merely running in circles. The new states have only succeeded in substituting inefficient African oppression for the more sophisticated and sometimes paternal forms of European colonial oppression. While they claim to be revolutionary, they find inspiration in historical determinism, leaving little latitude for revolutionaries who wish to change the predetermined course of events.

The African intelligentsia is not responding to this dilemma with a coherent political philosophy. Instead, it has produced a set of fragmentary, inconsistent, vague, and contradictory ideas.

Some African leaders, such as Nkrumah and Nasser, whose revolutionary theory conceives of history as the spirit's progress toward liberation, have adopted an outlook similar to that of the early Utopian socialists. They believe in some kind of transcendental justification of the free spirit in necessary rebellion against all restraints. Then there are leaders such as Senghor and Nyerere, who insist on an organic African reality in culture, law, politics, and economic development. Other African elites, like Fanon and Touré, portray an Africanism which takes the form of a new romantic idealism; they conceive of African national problems as contests between forces of good and evil—the evil of the colonial environment and an undefined African good. This group calls for total Africanization in society, politics, and culture.

There are those Africans, such as Kenyatta, who are not quite as immersed in romanticism. They retain the idea of progress and incline toward a moderate liberalism which is optimistic in its faith in the African future. And there are leaders, such as Bourguiba and Houphouet-Boigny, who are impressed by utilitarian economic and political theory, who dissent from the radical rebellion against colonial culture and international heritages.

The contemporary African revolutionary temper is trying to resolve the problem of Africa's history by pouring it into a dialectical mold; its spirit is often immoderate, negativist, racially self-conscious, and deterministic.

The African argument over history is, at best, a shallow spiritual probing for a basis of faith in the past; at worst, it is a prostitution of history leading to cynical politics, or a surrender to an uncritical Marxist interpretation of the world. In the face of all these contradictions, it is well to remember that Africa has not yet experienced herself in full form.

ILLUSTRATIONS OF
AFRICAN REVOLUTIONARY THOUGHT

Frantz Fanon

Born in Martinique, but Algerian by naturalization, Frantz Fanon is an articulate exponent of contemporary African revolutionary thought. He was a leading political theoretician in the Algerian independence movement, as well as one of the principal activists in the Algerian Liberation Front.

In Fanon's philosophy of revolution, de-colonization is a violent dialectical process. It will create a synthesis of new men with fresh mentalities. Fanon calls for a complete overhaul of the old system of relationships between nations, a process which he describes as having a "political philosophical objective which seeks to conform to the dictum: The last shall be the first."[1] This idea has the logical consequence that the "last" must be made to "climb the well-known steps which characterize an organized society, and they can only triumph through violence."[2]

Fanon says that the world of colonialism is divided into two parts: that of the colonialist and that of the native. The former is a good one, with values, and comfort. The latter, according to the colonialists, is a world without values; it is, in fact, a negation of values. The colonialists see the native as a destructive element—destroying, deforming, or disfiguring whatever comes his way. The result of this colonial categorizing is that the native is dehumanized.

Yet, the moment the native realizes "that his life, his breath, his beating heart are the same as those of the settler," a "new, revolutionary assurance of the native" appears.[3] In a sense, the appearance of the colonial settlers caused the death of aboriginal society, which in turn brought on a widespread native cultural lethargy.

In spite of all this, the native never looks to violence as an absolute line of action, but rather sees it as a useful tool because it unifies diverse peoples. It is a cleansing force which frees the native from fear, inferiority, despair, and inaction. It restores native self-respect and dignity. Fanon points out that in every case the great figures of colonized peoples have led national resistance movements against foreign domination. He attributes the breakdown of the colonial epoch to native resistance, either through violent popular revolution, or through popular action and unrest which have acted as a brake on the excesses of colonialism. The native intellectual has been forced to accept certain essential Western values; deep in every intellectual's mind, Fanon observes, one can find a "vigilant sentinel ready to defend the Graeco-Latin pedestal."[4] But during the struggle for independence when the native intellectual comes into contact with his own peoples, all the Mediterranean ideas of human rights, beauty, and clarity vanish—they become worthless to him because they are irrelevant to the struggle.

Fanon believes that self-criticism is a traditional African institution, and is not typical only of the West. In the villages of North and West Africa, public communal self-criticism is quite common. Thus, individualism is the first Western value to fall in the process of de-colonization. According to Fanon, it has been hammered into the reluctant mind of the intellectual by the bourgeoisie. But after the revolution it will be replaced by communalism, and, henceforth, the interest of one will be the interest of all. In short, the individualist motto, "Look out for yourself," will be forbidden.[5]

To Fanon, truth serves a pragmatic purpose in the nationalist cause. To the native, truth is that which is bad for the settler. It is that which spurs the breakdown of the colonial era. It is that which creates the nation, protects the native, and destroys the settler.

Every native who takes up arms against the colonialists is, according to Fanon, a part of the nation which will spring to life as soon as the old regime is destroyed. Programs of violence, organized by the nationalist leaders and carried out by the people, make it possible for the masses to understand social truths. Without violence, without knowledge of the politics of action, there is nothing but a "fancy dress parade and the blare of trumpets."[6] The result of a nonviolent struggle is a waving of flags and a few reforms at best. The masses will remain at the bottom, unredeemed.

Fanon claims that most of the African Nationalist parties do not try to give the country any specific objective. They merely hope that the movement will continue indefinitely, thus perpetuating their position. Nationalist parties make use of spontaneous rebellions and revolts, but they make no effort to lead or organize them. Though they wish the rebellions to continue, they do not openly support them, leaving their conduct to the spontaneous ebb and flow of mass passions.

Nationalist party politics are described by Fanon as a struggle between the wish to destroy colonialism and the wish to be in friendly agreement with it. Schisms which weaken the movement develop between intellectual and activist elements of the party.

Fanon clearly recognizes the problem of building a national consciousness, however, and identifies several of the cleavages which make such an undertaking difficult. He asserts that the native bourgeoisie is split from the masses because of its identification with the European bourgeois colonial elements. This split often results in the destruction of the native middle class, a downfall which may be hastened by the ties with its Western mentor.

The native middle class clamors for nationalization, not because it will help the new states, but because it means the transfer of state control into native hands. The middle class then acts as the intermediary between the new states and colonial capitalism. This makes the native bourgeoisie incapable of fullfilling its historical role as a national bourgeoisie, for it turns the new states toward Europe rather than inward.

Fanon feels that since the African national bourgeoisie is incapable of matching the accomplishments of its European counterpart—namely, the creation of a large industrial proletariat—it is harmful to progress and should be abolished. He feels that questions as to whether the bourgeois phase of national development can be stopped should be answered not by rhetoric but by revolutionary action. He is disgusted with the rise of dictatorships in the trans-national phases of national development. He believes that this will lead to a betrayal of the people. Democracy is a form of government which places power in the hands of a mass party, not of a single leader. A country that is genuinely interested in answering the questions that history puts to it, that intends to develop the mind of its citizens, as well as its cities, surely needs a "trustworthy" political party.[7]

Only a decentralized party can bring life to all the regions of a state. The party must educate the masses politically, for it is only through education that the entire nation can be bound into a cohesive reality. A leader who provides nationalism alone fails in his mission. On the other hand, a blind demand to meet social and political needs without humanism is also destructive of national goals. To Fanon, the nation—the true nation—is one in which all the people participate through a mass party.

Political parties, therefore, must have their roots in the masses and must be direct expressions of popular will. He believes that for a party to be a true party, it must not be merely an administration transmitting governmental orders. His unbounded and unquestioning faith in the people is deeply rooted in a strong sense of mass democracy, a conviction that popular welfare should be the objective of government and party action, not its victim.

Fanon feels that a national culture not only rehabilitates the nation, but is also necessary for revolutionary change in the native and his society. He warns, however, that the historical necessity which compels Africans to speak of a continental cultural unity is an illusion which will lead them into a blind alley. He believes that there cannot be two identical African national cultures, nor can there ever be a continental "Black Culture" which will unite all the states of Africa.[8] He advances the idea that those who believe in the possibility of creating a black culture for all Africa forget that "niggers" are disappearing with the dissolution of colonial political and economic control and white supremacy. It is not around the homogeneous characteristics of black men that cultural unity can rally, but rather around the popular struggle which all the new African states have used to attain independence and a measure of national unity. The absolute requirement for such continental consciousness is a willingness on the part of all the states to commit themselves to the complete liberation of all Africa through joint popular struggles against all forms of colonialism and foreign domination.[9]

Fanon abhors Europe and European values precisely because he sees them as the negation of the very bases of all humanity. He protests that when "he searches for man in the technique and style of Europe, he sees only a succession of the negation of man and an avalanche of murders."[10] Europe has stifled humanity in the name of so-called spiritual values, and as a result men today are "swaying between the atomic and the spiritual disintegration."[11] He advises the Third World not to try to catch up with the West, but rather to "go forward all the time, night and day, in the company of man."[12] He concludes:

> It is a question of the Third World starting a new history of Man, a history which will have regard to the sometimes prodigious theses which Europe has put forward . . . Humanity is waiting for something other from us than such an imitation . . . But if we want humanity to advance a step further . . . then we must invent and make discoveries . . . For Europe, for ourselves, and for humanity, . . . comrades, we must turn over a new leaf, we must work out new concepts, and try to set afoot a new man.[13]

Kwame Nkrumah

In his writings, the former first president of Ghana has attempted to provide a philosophical interpretation of African revolution. He believes that society and ideology are generically related.[14] Ideology arises from the social milieu. A revolutionary ideology, according to Nkrumah, does not merely express the wish that a present social order should be abolished; it also seeks to create and maintain a new order. Societal ideology thus expresses itself in political, moral, and social terms.

Nkrumah states that progress from communalism to socialism could have been achieved in Africa through normal processes of reform, since the underlying assumptions and principles are the same. But, as in Europe, the communalistic societies have gone through feudalistic, capitalistic, and colonialistic stages of development. Consequently, revolution is indispensable to the establishment of socialism because the antecedent socio-political structures have been animated by principles which negate the assumptions of socialism.

The substance of Nkrumah's professed ideology is consciencism, which he defines as that "philosophical standpoint" based upon the African conscience and indicating the way that progress is forged out of "conflict in that conscience." In his writings and speeches he has attempted, with little success, to work his way out of this tautology and to develop an independent philosophy of African revolution.

Basic to philosophical consciencism is the concept that man is endowed with individual value, dignity, and integrity. He is a spiritual being, without original sin. This African conception of man imposes "duties of a socialist kind." The individual, as Nkrumah sees him, has both idealistic and materialistic tendencies which are in tension rather than equilibrium. He believes that traditional African values of communal concern and cooperation will harmonize man's inner conflicts.

If socialism is true to its purpose, it will recreate the humanist, egalitarian, pre-colonial African past. It will prevent the spread of class privilege and destroy the remnants of "colonial mentality." Where individuals are treated as *ends* and not as *means,* according to philosophical consciencism, there occurs a transition to politics. Philosophical consciencism preserves the ethical principle of initial human value.

Nkrumah asserts that the humanist traditions embedded in African society should form the basis of any modern cultural synthesis. Communal elements must prevent excessive individualism in economic matters, and the community must exercise control over alien influences. The traditional African humanist and cultural base must be preserved.

Pan-Africanism is Nkrumah's expression of consciencism on a continental scale. Unable to survive alone in the hostile world, the states of Africa will find safety and well-being within common political and economic institutions.

The primary threat to the fledgling states is neo-colonialism. This odious phenomenon, with diffuse religious, ideological, cultural, political, and particularly economic techniques, attempts to deny the African states the reality of freedom. The consequences of such factors as the rise and fall of world demand for their products, the world monetary system, the influx of foreign capital, and unilateral or multilateral foreign aid are the exploitation of the African peoples and the expansion of the gap between the rich and the poor.

Pan-Africanism promises freedom from neo-colonialism. When brought to fruition, it will offer a framework within which the agricultural and industrial sectors of Africa can expand rapidly, and allow the Africans freedom from world capitalism. Collectively, the Africans can control a great non-aligned force in world politics to promote their aspirations and the hopes of all oppressed peoples in the world.

Gamal Abdel Nasser

President Nasser of Egypt agrees with Nkrumah that revolutions and the philosophies behind them arise from the social and historical milieu of the people. To Nasser, the story of national struggle contains no "gaps filled with nothingness; neither does it feature any surprises that leap into existence without introduction."[15] Every national struggle and revolution has popular foundation.

Nasser speaks of two revolutions: political and social. The goal of the former is self-determination; thus, it attempts to fight any kind of occupation or pressure coming from abroad. Its direct aims are to promote evacuation from the occupied lands. This is the phase of rejection of the colonialist rule. The goal of the latter is an end to class conflict; thus, it attempts to break the grip of monopoly which represents a threat to the underdeveloped countries. At the same time, in order to escape economic and psychological pressure, a policy of non-alignment must be followed. According to Nasser, states may not experience both revolutions at the same time; the political and social revolutions may be centuries apart.

The Egyptian people, he feels, must undergo the two revolutions simultaneously. Social revolution involves hate, dissension, and corruption, and intensifies class conflicts. It shakes values and principles and gives free rein to doubt, violence, and egoism. Its role is to eliminate class conflict. To achieve this, the people must have control over the capital as well as the production media. Land must be distributed, and equal opportunity must be provided for work, education, and social protection. Egypt is caught between two revolutionary millstones: one calling for unity, the other destroying it.

> When one of my comrades came to me saying "You want unity to face the English, but at the same time you allow the treason courts to continue their work," I listened to him with our great crisis in mind, the crisis of the millstones—a revolution on the one hand which obliges us to unite in one phalanx and to forget the past, and on the other hand, another revolution which demands that we restore lost dignity to our moral values by not forgetting the past. I might have replied that our only salvation lies, as I said before, in maintaining our speed of movement and our initiative, and our ability to travel through two revolutions simultaneously.[16]

Nasser's philosophy of a "triple sphere" within which Egypt must play its role as a nation is a revolutionary concept. He believes that fate has decreed a number of circles within which Egypt's historical destiny must be fulfilled: the Arab circle, the African circle, and the Islamic circle. His country should play a role in all three.

The Egyptian people, who constitute the link between Africa and the outside world, must play a role on the African continent. They cannot remain aloof from the conflict in Africa today between five million whites and two hundred million blacks.

> The Dark Continent is now the scene of a strange and excited turbulence: the white man . . . is trying to re-divide the map of Africa. We shall not, in any circumstance, be able to stand idly by in the face of what is going on . . .

> I will continue to dream of the day when I will find in Cairo a great African institute dedicated to unveiling to our view the dark reaches of the continent . . . and to sharing with others from all over the world the work of advancing the welfare of the peoples of this continent.[17]

Nasser sees no relevance to Egypt in Western democracy; for him it is merely a vehicle of capitalist expansion. While he voices

Marxist doctrines, he opposes a dictatorship of the proletariat. While he is intent on abolishing the classes that have traditionally dominated Egypt, he does not attempt to construct a classless society. While he asserts that he has no basic quarrels with Marxism, he does not tolerate a Communist party in Egypt.

Nasser says that democracy must operate in the daily life of the people, not just in such institutional manifestations as parliament and elections. He feels, however, that Egyptians are ill-prepared for the Western parliamentary institutions that the old regime had introduced to manipulate the masses for its own ends. These so-called democratic institutions were centers of political corruption. Thus, Nasser sees the necessity of a transitional period in which Egyptians can be educated in order to understand and use effectively the prerogatives of full citizenship. Instead of political freedom, Nasser emphasizes "social democracy," designed to abolish class distinctions of wealth and privilege.

Habib Bourguiba

President Habib Bourguiba of Tunisia combines the traits of a Western statesman with the emotional appeal of an Arab nationalist leader. Probably more than any other North African, he admits a continuing attachment to France; his statement, "I do not hate France, only colonialism," has become famous.

Bourguiba's blend of French and Muslim cultures is consistent with the Tunisian tradition of cultural accommodation and assimilation. This has colored his every action vis-à-vis the Western states—a desire to be respected by them and be accepted as an equal. It has also been a major determinant in the political and ideological course that Tunisia has taken since its independence in 1956. Bourguiba has emphasized:

> This consciousness [referring to the priority of the economic and social struggle] explains the mobilization of the Tunisian energies. It is not a mobilization that is directed against imaginary enemies, but rather towards constructive work, a rational organization of programs of action and a full exploitation of human possibilities and technical knowhow. This is the secret of Tunisia's advance and the method by which we will rapidly reach the stage all Tunisians hope for: a respectable position among the advanced countries. By this, I do not mean countries who, for appearances' sake, maintain splendid embas-

sies and build luxurious ministries in order to impress their visitors. I mean by "advanced" countries that have high standards of living.[18]

Bourguiba's revolutionary temper is a moderate one. This contrast with extreme Arab revolutionary thought is explained partially by the fact that Tunisia moved towards independence from France by means of negotiation rather than prolonged violence.

Bourguiba is neither a follower of a specific doctrine nor the creator of any. In this respect he emphasizes that he is neither a man of doctrine, nor feels a need for one. Bourguiba's concept of revolution is purely pragmatic. It is aimed at freeing his country from colonialism and from external pressures, but it is not in any way aimed at the destruction of capitalism.

Bourguiba's goals and aspirations are more like those of bourgeois nationalists than of revolutionaries. He hopes to improve the Tunisian standard of living through large-scale industrialization, irrigation projects, and land reform. This would open the way for the Tunisian middle classes to exercise the dominant role in the economy and society that the French *colon* played prior to 1956.

Bourguiba is more secular and Westernized than many other African leaders. But, because of the nature of Tunisian society, he is unable to translate the ideals of Western liberalism which he admires into reality. During the four years he spent as a political exile in Cairo (1945-49), Bourguiba remained unsympathetic to Egyptian and other forms of contemporary Arab political thought.

Bourguiba's strength is based both on his charismatic personality and on his talent for organization. However, he has unwittingly allowed himself to be separated from his people by overprotective, but not always loyal, counselors and admirers. His party, the Destourian Socialist, has organized an elaborate network of cells. Though his political machine is relatively less aggressive than Nasser's, it is more effective.

Julius Nyerere

For Nyerere, politics is the organization of consensus. Both within his state of Tanzania and on the continent of Africa, he assumes that the basis of this consensus exists. Nyerere speaks of the pre-colonial African characteristics of equalitarianism and humanism. With the attainment of independence, all Africans can regain these traditional political modes.

Because there is a basis of consensus within the state, Nyerere believes that the European "isms," as well as such notions as interest, coercion, and elites, are superfluous. The nation is a pre-existing reality coterminous with the state, which the party alone can represent. The party provides the space of freedom within which differences are reconciled through dialogue and consensus generated. After the party synthesizes the differences, however, no opposition can exist. Nyerere heralds democratic centralism in Tanzania.

As the state must be founded on consensus and protected against the evils of a pandering opposition, so must the African continent eventually be organized and isolated from alien vectors of political conflict. Only through organization of continental scope, Nyerere says, can Africans shield themselves from the cold war. He cites the Congo crisis as a warning against introducing cold war rivalries into Africa. Most important, Nyerere asserts, is the creation of a united African front in the conflict between the rich and poor states. The rich states, both capitalist and socialist, threaten vulnerable and poor African states by attempting to play off one against another. Nyerere says:

> I believe firmly that, just as unity was necessary for the achievement of independence in Tanganyika or any other nation, unity is equally necessary to consolidate and maintain the independence which we are now achieving in different parts of Africa.[19]

However, Nyerere's theme is for African states in the immediate future to accept economic and political diversity while striving for socialism. Moderate socialism, with state control and an egalitarian society, seems to be the essence of Nyerere's revolutionary aspirations.

Ahmed Sékou Touré

Like the chiliastic philosophies of many other African leaders, the Jacobinism of Ahmed Sékou Touré is predicated upon metaphysical assumptions of dubious consistency and relevance.[20] Touré defines true Guinean consciousness in terms of an effective motivation to improve the entire society. In the good society, says Touré, all the restraints wrought by colonialism will be replaced by this conscience of social justice.

Only Touré's party, the Parti Démocratique de Guinée, (P.D.G.), can usher in the good society; it alone embodies this pre-existent consciousness. Those who oppose the party are not evil, they are simply ignorant of the metaphysical verities that govern politics in Guinea. Touré concedes that in states with pronounced social and economic cleavages multi-party systems can exist. This, however, is not the case in Guinea, where development depends upon a party which insures the unity of all the people and the state.

Through the party and education, the individual and the collectivity are harmonized. There is no need to repeat the European experience of feudalism and capitalism in Guinea; the inherent moral stature of the true Guinean and revolutionary struggle by the party guarantee social equilibrium. The construction of a socialist society, rooted in the communal African past and guided by the vision of a Marxist heaven, can begin.

The revolutionary principles of the P.D.G. can be exported, however, only by the word, not by the sword. Guinea can function only as an example to the continent of Africa and the world. Touré lauds the Organization of African Unity as a bulwark against the pernicious encroachments of neo-colonialism. Guinea makes her presence felt in great power politics through the posture of "positive neutralism." While not damning the existing system of power politics, Guinea stands on moral grounds in refusing to take part in it. The word, "positive," affixed to neutralism, nonetheless implies an acceptance of responsibility towards mankind. Hence the staccatoed damnation of world events and personages which Touré unleashes periodically. The ostensibly Guinean principles of the P.D.G. seem to furnish him with an absolute criterion for judging the entire outside world.

Felix Houphouet-Boigny

Felix Houphouet-Boigny, President of the Ivory Coast, is one of the few African leaders who has attempted to chart a middle course between amiable relations with non-African states and with his continent. He believes that the Ivory Coast's associations with France, particularly, and with Africa will yield a new national social synthesis.

Houphouet-Boigny believes that Pan-Africanism is both a prerequisite for and a manifestation of real African progress.[21] The friendship and brotherhood of the African peoples will bring about a continental framework for co-operation. He looks to the potential leadership of the youth and to the new African personality which will transcend its primordial sentiments. But, he does not want to isolate the continent; the new African, rather than looking inward, would begin a dialogue between himself and the world. He would be sensitive to cultural, economic, and political influence coming from other continents.

Houphouet-Boigny condemns what he considers to be the parochialism of the African leaders who champion either national or continental autarchy; he has no sympathy for those who would build high walls around the African peoples. He states that agreements with great powers, ex-colonial states, and non-African regional groupings lie wholly within the Africans' interest.

Houphouet-Boigny feels that there is only one true African approach to international politics: "absolute neutrality." He has stated that his ambition in foreign policy is "the total neutrality of Africa." This can come about when there is peace among the African countries and between Africa and the other continents.

ONE-PARTY SYSTEMS

The domestic political environment in the new African states has been especially conducive to the emergence of small leadership elites who hold effective control of national affairs. Such centralization of power has had obvious effects on the structure and processes of African political life.

African nationalist leaders, around whom the anti-colonialist movements coalesced, are identified as the embodiment of their new states. Such a position inevitably leads to an over-concentration of personal power: the African leader becomes the government itself. This increase of personal power is partly the result of the lack of a trained bureaucracy. In the absence of competent subordinates, African leaders assume personal responsibility for governmental action and are bound to accumulate extensive personal powers. Such inordinate power concentrated in the hands of a leader and his personal clique leads to a policy-making process which is nearly always arbitrary. Without a competent bureaucracy, policy decisions are made without regard for differing points of view. There is often little opportunity for the transmission of information which does not support the position of the leadership elite. It is obvious that policy decisions made in such an operational vacuum bear no relevance to actual situations and are destructive of manifest objectives.

The popular pressures and emotions which African nationalist leaders fostered and molded for use in ousting the colonial regimes are now being directed against them as heads of governments. A major anti-colonialist issue was that the imperial powers were inhibiting material and social progress in Africa. The masses were led to believe that once the colonial regime was destroyed, near-Utopian conditions would prevail. Progress was very often viewed as the justification for independence, but just what did the Africans mean by "progress?"

This is a relevant and important question precisely because the Africans themselves do not seem to know what they mean. Development and progress are used interchangeably; progress is equated with industrialization, with prosperity, and with human welfare, and is the over-all spirit behind African attempts at nation-building. But, operationally, progress often means nothing more than the very conspicuous—but generally quite useless—construction of public works projects.

Enormous popular pressures for such visible, but irrelevant, achievements force the governments of the new states into a costly diversion of scarce funds which could be used more effectively in other developmental programs. When faced with a choice between a series of bush hospitals or a superhighway between provincial capitals, the government usually chooses the road, even if there is an insufficient number of vehicles to justify its construction. It is the immediate and material symbols of progress that impress Africans.

But it is not unusual for newly-independent peoples to look to their nationalist leaders for guidance during the post-independence transition period. These leaders stress national and political unity as being necessary for development, and in doing so, excoriate factionalism. But unity must be predicated upon an active national consciousness, a broad popular consensus, and a homogeneity which are missing from the African scene.

Ethnic, geographical, social, economic, and historical diversity in the African states lead to political regionalism which is in direct contradiction to unity. Factionalism abounds, and the various groups too often think and act in mutually exclusive "we" and "they" terms. The spirit of coalition and co-operation is generally lost under such conditions; democracy is interpreted as majority rule with minority exclusion. It is obvious that such assumptions can easily lead to a destructive political in-fighting and to governmental suppression of the opposition. Although it is the task of the nationalist governments to unite rival factions, men in power are greatly tempted to impose a consensus from above, a consensus which generally reflects their own or their party's position.

In adopting the most obvious of democracy's tenets, majority rule, Africa has overlooked its corollary: minority participation in the decision-making processes. Because of the heterogeneity of the African states and the general preoccupation with factional interests, it is absolutely essential, not only for the sake of the democratic process, but also for the continued existence of the state, that minorities be allowed to participate meaningfully in government policy-making. Yet this is not the case.

In some African states, rival and opposition groups are suppressed simply because they challenge the "in" position of the ruling party. Yet, it could also be argued that the reason they challenge the ruling party's position is precisely because they are totally excluded from the government. Where coalitions and inter-party co-operation are generally ignored, the opposition is forced to turn to obstructionalism, if not outright revolution or secession.

In such a political environment, the uneducated masses play a primary role. How to claim progress—or the lack of it—as the sole doing of the party in power becomes the main concern of the ruling and opposing groups. The African passion for conspicuous material extravagances forces the nationalist leaders to vie for popular support by diverting resources and capital into projects which may bear no relevance to actual national development, but which might very well mean the difference between being in or out of power. No matter how well-intentioned a party might be, as long as minorities and opposition groups are excluded from policy participation, it will almost inevitably be caught up in a round of irrelevancies. Eventually the party may find it necessary to establish itself as the only legal party, thereby further distorting the political process.

It should be obvious that such situations are highly unstable. Instead of actual elections, polling will be reduced to simple referendum. Real changes in government will be possible only through coups d'état and assassination. The ruling groups will resort to further suppression in an effort to retain control. But, in so doing they completely transform the democratic concept of rule by majority into an authoritarian tyranny of a self-declared majority, actual or not. The pattern is quite familiar in the twentieth century, and it is being repeated over and over again in the new African states.

Apologists for one-party statism in Africa assert that the exigencies of nation-building require authoritarian methods. They imply that once development, national unity, and social well-being are accomplished, the means used to attain these goals will be replaced. This is clearly wishful thinking. One-party dictatorships in Africa result from a narrow concept of democracy incorrectly applied to a pluralistic society. They are a new total distortion of the democratic ideal and are destructive of both democratic means and democratic ends. Such authoritarian patterns, once established, will become firmly enmeshed in a web of vested interests. As long as African leaders fail to develop the instruments of legitimacy for the exercise of power, African governments will not enjoy political stability. The life span of regimes will be determined by the ability of a ruling group to marshall more forces than its opposition. The proper use of instruments of legitimacy would link the ruler and ruled and institutionalize relationships with the policy. In the absence of such a contractual arrangement, the street and bullet will continue to constitute the principal links between government and people.

It is unreasonable to expect that such an apparatus of anti-democratic means would cease to exist once the immediate necessities of national development were overcome. On the contrary, they would be in more firm control than ever. Yet, this is precisely the error the apologists make when they close their eyes to the realities of the African situation.

Since the general tendency in the new African states is in

the direction of one-party control, it is imperative that the West understand its meaning and the factors causing it. Only then can African political life be clearly understood and, perhaps, dealt with more effectively.

APPARENT DIRECTIONS OF AFRICAN
REVOLUTIONARY THOUGHT

The African intelligentsia is revolting against the philosophy of things as they are, things as they were, and things as they are destined to be. Africa is caught between immovable objects—tribalism and tradition; and irresistible forces—nationhood and modernization. Africa is like a body with a wounded soul in search of a spirit. The wound of Africa is too deep for first aid treatment; the body of Africa is too weak for major surgery—yet that is precisely what Africa needs.

Africa has not yet come to terms with the question of national destiny. A single group or community in every state dominates over all others. National morale is at a low ebb, and the nascent feelings of public responsibility search desperately for a reason to justify their existence. National elites are untroubled by incompatibility of ideas; they are self-conscious and are afraid that they might not measure up to their Western counterparts. At its present stage, the African protest movement is fundamentally destructive. African leaders argue about principles, not interests; about procedures, not substance. To them, the gesture is of greater significance than the result.

There are no co-ordinated or stabilized societies in today's Africa. The African individual has not acquired a sense of political freedom or dignity. He has the desire, but not the will, to improve his lot in life. The diverse components of a given African society remain unintegrated.

There is a fear of freedom in Africa. The native thinker's intellect is subservient to his pride; hence, his intellectual and moral dignity is undermined. He has a pathological resentment of white domination, and a pitiful yearning to prove to himself his own dignity and worth. Yet, he still feels the lash in the person of the white man.

While the independence of the new states constitutes a revolutionary element in the international system, African revolutionary thought is desperately searching for roots. Because they are not yet found, the African fails to engage in necessary long-range programs. In attempting to undo colonial wrongs, he concentrates solely on the negativism of anti-colonialism, and thus prejudices his capacity for positive action.

In its choice of enemies, African revolutionary thought is open to further question. African leaders draw on an inexhaustible reservoir of evil spirits—neo-colonialism, "American imperialism," and Western "domination." To the African, the real enemies —political "cannibalism," economic inefficiency, and social weaknesses—are too dangerous to deal with.

Because the African lacks faith in himself, it is inconceivable to him that he could be held in high esteem by others. Hence, when he is treated as an equal, he immediately becomes mistrustful. The new African has emancipated himself from without, but he has a long way to go before he liberates himself from within.

African revolutionary thought, therefore, is contradictory in nature. The rapid emergence of independent African states in the international system, their impact on the rest of the world, and the superficial African institutional changes have blended an old setting with a new environment.

Thus, the African revolutionary temper expresses itself in three ways. First, in its real sense, it is anti-colonial. Second, in its theoretical sense, it seeks to create something new out of a blend of external influence and traditional domestic realities. Third, in its romantic sense, it dreams of continental political unity—the establishment of a United States of Africa.

The new Africa is an amalgam of deep-rooted historic traditions and turbulent historic forces. The present African dialogue manifests both the death throes of a culture and the type of development commonly antecedent to a process of change and adjustment.

Four basic principles have begun to emerge within the African process of change and adjustment. First, the leaders of Africa are attempting to further freedom through nationalism. Secondly, they are seeking progress through a special kind of socialism. Thirdly, on less well-defined principles, they are searching for order, dignity, and self-expression through federalism or

Pan-Africanism. Finally, they are pursuing security through neutralism.

NOTES

1. See Frantz Fanon, *The Wretched of the Earth* (New York: The Grove Press, 1963), p. 30.

2. *Ibid.*

3. *Ibid.*, pp. 36-37.

4. *Ibid.*, p. 37.

5. *Ibid.*, p. 38.

6. *Ibid.*, p. 117.

7. *Ibid.*, p. 148.

8. *Ibid.*, p. 188.

9. *Ibid.*, pp. 188-189.

10. *Ibid.*, p. 253.

11. *Ibid.*, p. 252.

12. *Ibid.*, pp. 254-255.

13. *Ibid.*, p. 255.

14. See Kwame Nkrumah, *Africa Must Unite* (New York: Frederick A. Praeger, 1963); *Ghana: The Autobiography of Kwame Nkrumah* (London: Thomas Nelson and Sons, 1957); *I Speak of Freedom: A Statement of African Ideology* (New York: Frederick A. Praeger, 1961); *Consciencism* (London: Heinemann, 1964); and *Neo-Colonialism: The Last Stage of Imperialism* (London: Thomas Nelson and Sons, 1965).

15. Gamal Abdel Nasser, *Egypt's Liberation: The Philosophy of the Revolution* (Washington, D.C.: Public Affairs Press, 1955), p. 17.

16. *Ibid.*, pp. 44-45.

17. *Ibid.*, pp. 110-111.

18. Habib Bourguiba, *Building a New Tunisia* (Tunis: Secretariat of Information, January 12, 1961), p. 11.

19. Paul E. Sigmund, Jr., (ed.), *Ideologies of the Developing Nations* (New York: Frederick A. Praeger, 1963), p. 205.

20. See Ahmed Sékou Touré, *L'Afrique et la Révolution*, Tome 13. [This publication carries neither date nor place of publication. It appears that it is a publication of the Republic of Guinea.]

21. See *Discours Prononcé par Monsieur le Président de la République Felix Houphouet-Boigny* (Korhogo: Service de Presse, Presidence de la Republique, May 7, 1965).

BIBLIOGRAPHY

ABRAHAM, WILLIE E. *The Mind of Africa*. Chicago: The University of Chicago Press, 1962.

CAMERON, JAMES. *The African Revolution*. New York: Random House, 1961.

FANON, FRANTZ. *The Wretched of the Earth*. New York: Grove Press, 1963.

————. *Pour la Révolution Africaine*. Paris: Francois Maspero, 1964.

————. *L'an V de la Révolution Algérienne*. Paris: Francois Maspero, 1966.

KAPLAN, MORTON A. (ed.). *The Revolution in World Politics*. New York: John Wiley and Sons, 1962.

KAUTSKY, JOHN H. (ed.). *Political Change in Underdeveloped Countries*. New York: John Wiley and Sons, 1962.

LEWIS, WILLIAM H. (ed.). *New Forces in Africa*. Washington, D.C.: Public Affairs Press, 1962.

NASSER, GAMAL ABDEL. *Egypt's Liberation: The Philosophy of the Revolution*. Washington, D.C.: Public Affairs Press, 1955.

NKRUMAH, KWAME. *Consciencism*. London: Heinemann, 1964.

SEGAL, RONALD. *African Profiles*. Baltimore, Md.: Penguin Books, 1963.

SIGMUND, PAUL E. (ed.). *The Ideologies of the Developing Nations*. New York: Frederick A. Praeger, 1963.

TOURE, AHMED SEKOU. *L'Afrique et la Révolution*. [This publication carries neither date nor place of publication. It appears that it is a publication of the Republic of Guinea.]

5 •

Freedom
through Nationalism

As a primarily emotional ideology, nationalism aims at some form of socio-political union of people who share common values and requirements. One of its prime functions is to organize a consensus on goals and purposes and to mobilize the society in the pursuit of those goals.

Nationalism has been traditionally identified with the already existing socio-politico-economic groupings called nation-states, and it is further linked to the concept of national consciousness, a feeling of belonging to an existing unity. National consciousness provides a people with a sense of cohesion and a willingness for sacrifice which is necessary to the development, maintenance, and assertion of viable nation-statehood. Without some degree of nationalism, the community's interests and goals cannot be expressed effectively, and the community is likely to be divided by factionalism, with chaos as the eventual result.

Contemporary African nationalism takes the form of an intense, but disorganized groping toward a modern, idealized future. The confused diversity of its expression is in part due to the African tendency to romanticize a misty tribal past. It may seem to be a distinct variation of the basic emotion of nationalism, for it seeks to *create* states where previously there have been none. Its primary aim is to integrate a territorially-defined but internally-divided entity into a cohesive, coherent unity which can then proceed to the problems of development, social welfare, and national expression.

THE NATURE OF AFRICAN NATIONALISM

The new states of Africa are not the offspring of Congolese, Arab, Kenyan or other native nationalities, but rather of Western European, American, and Russian power politics, with the United Nations often acting as an international midwife. In most cases, a given concept of nationality is incongruent with the political boundaries of a particular state. Lacking operationally-effective political institutions and organizations, the African states are composed, in an analytic sense, of two co-existing groups: the ruling class and the masses.

The modern concept of the nation-state did not reach Africa until it was imported by the European colonial powers during the late nineteenth century. Individual aspirations were previously confined to either a tribe, a religious sect, or a town, and even today the ideas of national community and statehood have not yet found their place in the African frame of reference. The African masses remain indifferent to anything outside their immediate surroundings; provincialism and tribalism continue to govern their attitudes toward the outside world. Cultural and social homogeneity, which could fuse and mold the diverse elements of society into a national community, are lacking.

African nationalism does not receive most of its dynamics from a well-developed sense of belonging to a specific and distinct cultural unit which seeks to advance and maintain itself. It is instead primarily a movement of peoples who are racially conscious, must prove their equality with the long-dominant whites, have been introduced to the benefits of modernization and education, and passionately desire to create new and dynamic political and cultural entities from their homogeneous groupings. It has arisen, at least in part, as an expression of elements of society who wish to rid themselves of foreign domination, to organize and control their own governments, and to be responsible for the development of their own national system. It seeks to create a common consciousness, part of which may be based on racial factors, part on common experience with a colonial enemy, and a great deal of which is based on a real or imagined similarity of values derived from some actual or mythical greatness in the past.

In the Western world, nationalists spoke for political entities that existed. They started from a basic cohesion and solidarity to which they tried to give effective expression that had been lacking. In contrast, the African nationalists are faced with the task of creating not only the nations of which they speak, but also the emotions, the loyalties, and cohesions which animate nations. It is necessary for them to create not only the finished products, but also the raw materials. Africa's nationalist leaders all claim to speak for some body of people, but it can be asked with justice whether or not such a group actually exists. They demand self-government and self-expression, but the "self" which is to governed and expressed remains amorphous and undefined.

The primary goal of the nationalists is the creation of stable nation-states, and it remains almost completely unaccomplished, despite the proliferation of independent African states since the breakdown of the colonial empires. The colonial powers set in motion great forces of change, but they failed to provide form or direction; they did not create nations, for that was not their goal. However, it is questionable whether the colonial powers could have left viable nations behind them, even if they had so intended. The colonial administrations had rapidly undermined the traditional African societies. The task of replacing the old with something concrete and immediately relevant was left for the nationalist leaders and is the task which remains.

The African nationalists first sought "independence." From the West, Africans had learned of the notions of the self-determination of peoples, of material progress and well-being, and of political freedom from domination. Having asked why Africa should be excluded from these rights, they demanded independence. But the independence which Africans sought was viewed as an absolute, immutable state of being. Independence was seen as the "Good Fairy" who, with a single wave of her magic wand, would erase the bane of colonialism and leave Africa free to find and express her own identity. Once the colonial powers were ousted, everything injurious and evil would leave with them, and the ideal would coincide with the African unity. From such a conception of independence (the known, but not assimilated democratic ideals of the West), and the injustices of colonialism, there arose the anti-colonialist attitude which would prove to be the building and driving force of African nationalism.

ANTI-COLONIALISM

Almost immediately, the new African elites that colonialism had created began to search their societies for principles and values which could be wedded to their own anti-colonialist idealism. Such a combination would serve the double purpose of creating a rationale for their nationalist desires and a mass support for the expression of their position. The elites both discovered and invented, in a past both real and mythical, a set of concepts which could be used to build the idea of the "African personality." This African personality was supposed to represent the essential uniqueness of African experience and society.

African nationalism, rooted primarily in anti-colonialism, needed something positive which could structure the principally negative movement against the colonial powers. It needed something which could give purpose, direction, and force to the drive for independence. The positive factors which developed from the search for an African personality included notions of communal co-operation, racial equality, individual freedom, human dignity, and personal expression and fulfillment.

All African nationalist movements based themselves on such concepts. They asserted vigorously that these characteristics were intrinsic to African society and the birthright of all Africans. During the colonial period, the continent as a whole had been denied these rights by the dominant Europeans; it had been barred from development and self-expression by the colonial regimes. The nationalist leaders loudly and continuously proclaimed that the time had finally come for Africa to regain control of its destiny so that Africans could find the free expression that had been denied them for so long.

African nationalist leaders decided that the greatest strength of their societies lay in the traditional emphasis on communal co-operation. Each individual was seen as the product of a traditional order emphasizing co-operation, and each had a definite place in that order. Security and expression were found not in the individual, but rather in the collectivity. Colonialism has atomized this traditional order through exploitation. The resurrection of the African personality was seen as an absolute necessity which would be achieved by destroying colonialism and all its by-products.

During the colonial period, Africans were denied racial equality. Nationalists claimed that this enforced inferiority stifled African creativity and dynamism. They resented the barriers of white superiority which barred them from participating in the colonial administration and society. As their strength developed, the nationalists demanded equality more and more vociferously. Africa would prove itself if only given the opportunity; whites thought blacks inferior only because whites had been able to thoroughly dominate blacks. Gradually, the drive for acceptance and racial equality developed into the concept of Black Africa or *negritude*. Negro racial characteristics were proclaimed to be the framework of a unique personality, something to be proud of, not to be hidden beneath a cloak of shame. What began as an attempt to give the African a sense of personal worth and self-respect rapidly changed into an emotional reaction to white domination which could easily be twisted and distorted into black racism and black extremism.

As the basic ingredient of African nationalism, anti-colonialism continues to serve two primary functions. As it did in the past, it continues to provide unity and support necessary for a successful independence movement in areas still under colonial domination; and it continues to provide the perceived common threat which nationalist leaders can invoke to preserve their domestic and international positions once independence has been achieved.

It was stated earlier that the African states gained their independence at a time when sovereignty had become compromised by the technological necessities of interdependence. Self-sufficiency was no longer possible, no matter how passionately sought. As the vaunted ideals of the nationalist movements were compromised by the realities of the situation, ambitions remained unfulfilled and the new states were beset by acute problems of development.

While they were still colonial peoples, African nationalists had something specific, concrete, and immediately apparent on which they could blame virtually everything. The colonial regime was held responsible for disease, poverty, oppression, illiteracy—all the ills of African society. The nature of colonialism was portrayed as solely exploitative; Africans were the victims of injustice on a continental scale.

By concentrating their fire on the colonial powers, the nationalists were able to arouse the degree of popular sentiment and support necessary for the political revolution that would put them in power. They rode into office on waves of passionate anti-colonialism, but their promises of a bright future were yet to be satisfied.

The logic of anti-colonialism promised that once independence was won, all barriers to justice, freedom, and progress would be demolished. The promised land of the nationalist's dreams would be easily at hand. When this did not prove to be the case, social cohesion began to break down almost immediately. The unity achieved in the face of the common enemy was threatened, and with it, the very existence of the new states and their nationalist regimes.

Faced with failures, frustrations, and incipient revolutionary activities as the facade of unity begain to disintegrate, the nationalist leaders had to do something to preserve what they had sought for so long. Because many of them had been bred on a Marxist-Leninist doctrine of imperialism, it was not unusual that they should turn to seek the image of a new foe which could serve a unifying purpose similar to that of anti-colonialism.

During the national liberation campaigns, colonialism was usually described by the nationalists as unjust economic domination and exploitation by European finance capital. Starting with the premise that capitalist interests controlled the colonial powers, it was then charged that the capitalist interests continued in a post-independence attempt to exert *de facto* political control by economic means. The nationalist leaders thus created a new bogeyman: *neo-colonialism*. They claimed that the independence and progress of the new states was threatened by continued foreign economic domination. This form of covert control was denounced as the direct cause of the immediate failures of the post-independence period.

Nationalist attitudes toward colonialism and neo-colonialism have provided the African leaders with an opportunity to apply a disproportionate amount of political strength both at home and abroad. By capitalizing on their colonial experiences and on the East-West split, they are able to magnify their own importance and to resist the enticements of both blocs. They simultaneously accept sorely needed development aid, explain away domestic problems, and strengthen their domestic political positions.

On the surface, African anti-colonialism is almost synonymous with anti-Westernism. But this is at least a partial misconception. At the same time that the new African states are passionately derogating the West, they are actively attempting to imitate Western achievements. Anti-colonialism provides a convenient screen for their contradictory and confused attempts to achieve what they believe to be the hallmark of modern statehood.

ILLUSTRATIONS OF AFRICAN NATIONALISM

Kwame Nkrumah

Both in his writings and during his tenure in office, Ghana's Kwame Nkrumah has always upheld nationalism as an indispensable means to his avowed socio-politico-economic ends of national achievement.[1] It is primarily the tool for effective manipulation of mass emotions in support of the leadership elite. Nkrumah feels that the African leaders must overcome the fear and apathy of the colonial years and effectively express the basic desire to be free of all forms of domination. It is the responsibility of the new African leadership to renew the natives' self-confidence and organize them for the tasks of self-government and national development.[2]

Nkrumah's model of struggle for national liberation involves three distinct but interconnected stages. The first is the ouster of the colonial regimes and the capture of political power by Africans, themselves. In this initial stage, the support of the masses is essential, for without mass support, a disgruntled intelligentsia could be easily handled by the colonial administration. Mass support must be mobilized throughout the colony, and nationalist sentiments must be voiced in as many ways as possible. With a unity of purpose thus assured, the colonial regime will be overwhelmed.

Once political independence is won, the nationalist leadership must turn to the creation of a political system based on their interpretation of the mass will. The fight for democratic freedom is one of consolidation and of defense against neo-colonialist intrigues aimed at regaining control of the fledgling state. Nationalist sentiments will provide, in this stage, the determination necessary to meet the difficult tasks of development and maintenance of a state encircled by a hostile world.

The third stage is one of complete social reconstruction along socialist lines. Ultimate nationalist goals of material well-being and individual freedom within the framework of a socialist collectivity are realized in this final stage of development, and not before.

Nkrumah postulates the ideal African society as one of complete and uncompromised independence within which "the free development of each is the condition for the free development of all." National consciousness is the unifying force which makes all this possible. The people are endowed with a mystique which elicits the necessary sacrifices. The national mystique serves to unite the people for the struggle against colonial domination and for the crises of independence. The revolutionary action which is necessary for the achievement of new social and political systems in the African states can be effective, according to Nkrumah, only if the nationalist groups actually represent the popular will.

Nkrumah's nationalist tenets result in a kind of authoritarian emphasis on nationality and unity. The evils of colonialism and neo-colonialism are called upon to put down the opposition, and to create the desire to work, and the willingness to make sacrifices for the state.

Nkrumah's first and most pressing requirement is to make the state of Ghana immediately relevant to the diverse citizenry of that artificially created political entity. A community has been postulated where there was none before, and nationalist passions are required to help make that community a practical reality.

Nkrumah's nationalism is intensely idealistic as well as pragmatic. It is intellectually rooted in a belief in the inherent right of all men to be free and equal. Yet, in application, these ideals are twisted and compromised. He has written:

> The emancipation of Africa is the emancipation of man. This requires two aims: first, the reinstitution of the egalitarianism of human society, and second, the logistic mobilization of all our resources toward the attainment of that reinstitution.[3]

He draws freely on the largely fictitious past greatness of the West African kingdm of Ghana, which he idealizes and romanticizes. The challenges facing modern Ghana, he states, will be met if the spirit of the past can be recaptured and harnessed to the needs of the present.

In common with the other African nationalists, Nkrumah finds it easy to cultivate Pan-African idealism. He argues that the creation of independent African states is not enough. Independence and development are not really possible for any African state unless all are united in the search for identical continental goals. Nkrumah is also convinced that an extended continental African state can ultimately have a nationalism of its own.

Some sort of nationalism is obviously necessary for progress and development in the African states, but it can be extremely destructive of the very ends it seeks if it is twisted by demagoguery. Nkrumah has been accused of such demagogic behavior by some Western critics, though perhaps prematurely, because the exigencies of national development in Africa are such that nationalist passion is essential. But it is also essential that nationalism be kept under control by those who foster it.

Gamal Abdel Nasser

A semblance of modern Egyptian nationalism began to manifest itself under Muhammed Ali in the early nineteenth century. The immediate consequences proved both tragic and inglorious. While under Muhammed Ali the way seemed clear to a bright future, subsequent Egyptian ambition and expansion alarmed the great powers of the time. There resulted a period during which Egypt gradually passed under Western domination, climaxed by British occupation in 1882.

Egypt's primary goal soon came to be that of ending British control. The tragedy of this situation lay less in the development of bitter feelings between Egypt and the West than in the evolution of nationalist attitudes that were naive, immature, resentful, and concerned only with forcing British withdrawal. Internal problems and national development were generally ignored. It has been argued that Egyptian nationalism would have been as bankrupt and narrow under almost any other conditions. Although this is a moot point, it is important to note that Egyptians have not enjoyed the benefit of cultural articulation of their movement through any great nationalist philosophies; they have had no Voltaire or Thomas Paine.

President Nasser's brand of nationalism is primarily a pragmatic response to the day-to-day conditions and situations of the Arab world. What was originally an anti-monarchist reform movement was later wedded to anti-colonialism and eventually expanded as a sort of Pan-Arabism when more and more African and Arab states became independent.[4]

In the middle 1950's, there was a tremendous upsurge of nationalist sentiment in the Arab world. It did not begin with Nasser; but through his propaganda machines, his technicians, and his aid to various Afro-Asian national liberation fronts, he has tried to strengthen it as an effective force for the extension of Egyptian influence.

Egyptians have traditionally considered themselves to be distinct from both the Arabs and the African Negroes. Only after they found the opportunity to spread Egyptian influence in the Arab world and throughout Africa did the Egyptians identify themselves with the Arabs and Africans. With the increasing pressures of overpopulation, the pattern of traditional Egyptian expansionism will probably continue.

Nasser became the symbol of successful Arab nationalism, however, because his regime in Egypt has the advantage of seniority. His example has served to inspire other Arab nationalists, but it most definitely has not controlled them.

Nasser's nationalism is linked to the ideal of sovereign independence for all Arabs. From this he has generalized Pan-Arabism, for he feels that only in a united Arab world can Arabs be truly free from the pressures of neo-colonialism. The combination of Pan-Arabism and socialism gives direction and purpose to Egyptian nationalist factions, while constant reminders of the threat of neo-colonialism keep them at least partially united under Nasser's control.

Nasserian nationalism may be seen as a representative expression of the historic Arab drive for independence and dignity. Independence brings with it *pro forma* sovereignty, but dignity remains elusive. Insofar as Nasser expresses the common aspirations of the Arabs, he remains an acceptable symbol. But his specifically Egyptian approach exacerbates age-old Arab antagonisms, with the result that Pan-Arabism has degenerated into a series of petty disputes and a maze of contradictions.

Egyptian and Arab nationalism is a useful tool in international politics for Nasser. Its anti-Western content places him within reach of a position of world-wide leadership. Its anti-colonialist emphasis provides a bond with the new sub-Saharan states, and Pan-Arabism can be easily generalized to fit the idealistic Pan-Africanism of Senghor and Nkrumah.

At home, Egyptian nationalism gives Nasser the support essential to the survival of his regime. At the same time, it helps to generate the dynamism needed to develop the state into a modern industrial society. Development requires human forces, as well as material resources, and nationalism offers a way to capitalize on both.

Habib Bourguiba

A more moderate alternative to Egyptian nationalism is employed in Tunisia by Habib Bourguiba.[5] Traditional Tunisian society retained its stability during the period of the French protectorate, and there was little opposition to French rule.

In 1934, a group of young, educated Tunisians, led by Bourguiba, founded the Neo-Destourian Party (recently renamed the Destourian Socialist Party). This party remained the most active nationalist party during the entire period prior to independence in 1956. It then assumed the government of an independent Tunisia. The party was the foremost vehicle of concerted Tunisian nationalism. A mass party, it rejected doctrinaire rigidity in favor of widespread appeal across the entire spectrum of Tunisian society. The party was endowed with sober leadership during the period before independence. It adroitly employed both legal and illegal methods, in response to French Tunisian policy's vacillation between liberal and oppressive. After prolonged negotiations with the French and a period of transition, the party legally came to power by constitutional means.

Tunisia emerged as an independent state with none of the seemingly irremediable factionalism which plagues most African states; consequently, the authoritarian techniques utilized have been minimal. Domestically and internationally, the Tunisian government has acted in a more moderate fashion than most of the new African governments.

Attempts were made to protect the domestic consensus which emerged from the pre-independence period. A program of light industrialization and improved agricultural techniques was initiated. Cautious steps were taken to secularize Tunisian society. In speeches, Bourguiba has always stressed the relationship between effort and reward; he carefully avoids raising exaggerated expectations while foretelling the benefits of diligence and education.

Bourguiba has pursued a foreign policy appropriate to Tunisia's status as a non-aligned, underdeveloped state. Although he rhetorically alludes to Maghrebian unity (a community of the northern tier of African states), and a sense of affinity with the Black African states, Bourguiba has repudiated Nasser's Pan-Arabist policies. In the Arab League, Tunisia has often opposed Egyptian hegemony. In the United Nations, the Tunisian delegation has pursued a consistently moderate course within the African bloc.

Bourguiba's pragmatic approach extends to his dealing with the bipolar powers. He has resisted the temptation to tread the precarious tightrope which Nasser walks; rather, he generally commits Tunisia to the West on ideological and substantive issues. He emphasizes his state's Western orientation, though he speaks with sympathy of underdeveloped states which profess communist ideologies. His policies have been devoid of that messianic nationalism which characterizes Egyptian and other African nationalisms.

Jomo Kenyatta

Jomo Kenyatta's public life is typical of the life of a passionate nationalist. He began his political career in Nairobi, Kenya, in 1920, as a member of the East African Association, and shortly thereafter he became secretary-general of the Kikuyu Central Association, a nationalist group which opposed British land policies and European occupation of the Kenyan highlands.[6]

After studying in Britain and the Soviet Union, Kenyatta joined Kwame Nkrumah, George Padmore, and others in founding the Pan-African Federation in 1945. In 1947, he became president of the Kenya African Union, a nationalist party which sought to gain popular support for the extension of African rights in Kenya, and eventual Kenyan independence.

With the outbursts of Mau-Mau violence in 1950, European settlers demanded Kenyatta's imprisonment for his alleged *de facto* leadership of the Mau-Mau. Kenyatta countered by demanding Kenyan self-government in the European democratic tradition. He tried to bring the racists under control and to assert his moderate position of leadership over the independence movement. The racial inequality of the colonial regime was an evil which had to be erased before Kenya could hope to progress to self-government, but there also had to be unity and moderation in the movement.

Though it was never conclusively proven that Kenyatta had ties with the Mau-Mau, he was arrested in 1952 and the next year was sentenced to seven years in prison for seditious and rebellious acts. After his trial, terrorism increased and the colonial government was forced to call in British troops to augment native forces in dealing with the guerilla bands. Kenyatta was released from prison in 1959, but was detained in virtual exile in a remote province and barred from political activity. By this time, the issue of Kenyatta's release and return to politics became the nationalists' strongest weapon against the colonial government. Popular pressure mounted, and the British were forced to acknowledge Kenyatta's position as leader of the nationalist group and to allow him to return openly to the political scene.

In March, 1960, the Kenya African National Union (KANU), was formed with Kenyatta as president. KANU's stated aims were self-government and independence for Kenya, gradual confederation of East Africa leading to a united regional state, and full participation in the Pan-African movement. Kenyatta's KANU is committed to the development of a democratic, socialist, and united Kenya. Through his continued ties with Pan-Africanism, Kenyatta has spoken constantly of the necessity of a united Africa if all states are to move together towards modernization. Kenyatta has expanded his aims to include regional organization of the East African states. He feels that such integration offers the best hope for immediate development and provides the firmest base for the construction of an eventual continental African state.

Kenyatta has been concerned primarily with the assertion of African dignity and rights in a world dominated by white men. Anti-colonialism served the general purpose of providing a base for nationalist action, but Kenyatta has always firmly rejected any tendency to twist it into a black racism. His goal is to build a free, modern, and multi-racial society in Kenya, and he has tried to follow a moderate course.

Leopold Senghor

Leopold Senghor conceives of nationalism as primarily a means of uniting the tribes and factions of Senegal in a common cause which will ultimately provide a basis for integration of the entire continent under Pan-Africanism.[7] It is not a parochial glorification of particularly Senegalese attributes, but an attempt to arrive at some general principles which can unite Senegal for the tasks of nation-building and serve as possible bases for eventual African federation.

For Senghor, the state and its political apparatus are the essential expressions of the will of the community and are designed to serve that community's needs. His aim has been to emphasize the similarities, common values, and shared needs which can bind Africa together, hoping to keep it from degenerating into internal disintegration and strife.

> The state is the expression of a nation; it is primarily a means of realizing the nation. Political history teaches us that the lack of organization of the state is a weakness that fatally engenders the disintegration of the nation. In the first phase of nation building, we must organize the public powers of the federal state and provide a structure to guarantee their authority and permanence. We must also define the program that will orient the action of these public powers. For only this will make of our various populations a *People*, a *Community*, where each individual will identify himself with the collectivity and vice versa. But the unanimity, the communion of souls is not enough. For the people to become a nation, the individual must grow as his standard of living and culture is raised.[8]

Senghor realizes that the greatest dangers to a nascent state come from internal divisions and factionalism which can rend it before it has a chance to develop as a cohesive community. His acquaintance with European democratic socialism has given him the basic guidelines that he feels he must follow to build a strong Senegal. But he never lost sight of the ultimate dream of union of all Black Africa, and is careful not to follow any policies of exclusivity that would prejudice that dream. In Senegal he is trying to develop an African consciousness that will serve his purposes in the creation of the state, but which can also be extended by the people to a larger community when the time comes to take steps toward African federation.

Senghor knows that a certain mystique and cultural identity are necessary for Senegal to develop and grow as a united state, but he is also aware of the difficulties that can arise when the mystique becomes too exclusive. His concept of *negritude* can serve to unite Senegal and other African states, but it can also be turned into a black racist extremism which would destroy all that he is trying to create.

From a classical French education, Senghor has absorbed French liberal ideals and a sense of history which make him aware that it is absolutely necessary to provide his people not only with a state apparatus, but also with a positive dynamism which will harness that apparatus to their interests.

AFRICAN NATIONALISM: AN ASSESSMENT

The nationalists' romanticized versions of past African greatness and of the traditional values of their societies include an idealized picture of individual freedom in a sort of pure, primitive democracy. Accepted Western symbols of status, wealth, power, and prestige are declared alien to Africa, having been introduced by the white colonialists who have caused a corruption of the African Personality and must be suppressed or destroyed.

The purely negative nature of anti-colonialism would, under any circumstance, give African nationalism a partial unity, but it would only be temporary. The positive emotionalism, in the form of promises of the future to be gained through evocation of the past, is designed to gain the long-term supportive consensus necessary for nation-building.

The nationalists constantly proclaim that the best of the old should be united with the best of the new. Yet, as they are faced with the practical problems of application and development, they are generally unconcerned with the retention of only that part of the old that is compatible with the creation of a modern, Western-type society. To arouse the people, a real or imagined past is invoked in symbolic language which appeals to the emotions. But the basic substance of nationalist action and the nature of nationalist ends are plainly rooted in the problem of transition and creation in the modern world.

On the emotional level, nationalism evokes a sense of self-respect which was unknown during the colonial period. It stimulates social solidarity and helps create a meaningful community to which diverse peoples can claim a common loyalty. It is of prime significance when it helps create the national unity of purpose and readiness for sacrifice which are required for development and even for survival. It is an attempt to express not what is, in fact, but what is perceived as desirable—what should be.

African nationalism ranges the full spectrum from tribal factionalism, the blind fanaticism of terrorist groups, and the white or black racism of absolute superiority, to supra-national Pan-Africanism. It is revolutionary. No two nationalist groups envisage the same ultimate goals, and their concepts of organization, development, and democracy are unclear. In some cases, nationalism is seen as a means of recapturing a romanticized history, while in others, its primary emphasis is on the immediate and future problems of building modern states. And yet in other cases, nationalism is seen as a means of creating a powerful and well-developed united continental African state which could act with great, but undefined, independence and influence in the world.

The nationalists are generally vaguely conscious of a feeling of belonging to some real or imaginary group. The problem of the nationalist leaders is to try to develop and channel these feelings into meaningful expressions which will lead to attainment of what they have seen to be desirable in their contacts with the West.

African nationalism is a refutation of what Europeans have been saying about Africans for centuries, and a way of proving that Africa can and will take its rightful place in the world. It offers a means of proving to the Africans, too, that their inferiority was not a fact, but an enforced colonial myth. Nationalism also provides part of the spirit and drive necessary for the achievement of what is seen as a specifically African well-being. And yet, nationalism in Africa cannot speak, as in the West, for nations already in being, but only for nations that exist in the hopes of the leadership elites.

African nationalists are fond of saying that by ridding their continent of colonial regimes, they are trying nothing less than to regain and reassert the dignity of the African individual. They appeal to the undefined, and perhaps undefinable, African Personality and to the concept of *negritude,* the supposed unifying forces behind African nationalism. They emphasize that the search for the African Way is an attempt to rediscover, recreate, and redefine what *has been,* in order to understand what *is,* and what is likely to be.

One way that the African can overcome his enforced inferiority in a white man's world is to exclude the white from black states, create Negro nations, develop modern Negro societies, and act in concert with other Negro states at home and abroad—in an effort to prove that Africans are just as competent as whites in anything they attempt. But the question is: to whom is the African trying to prove these things? To the white man or to himself? The inferiority which was forced upon the Africans left a deep emotional scar; it is causing them to assert repeatedly their nationalism today. They are attempting to prove that they really are what they are not: modern, progressive, independent, and free nation-states.

These facts give a visionary quality to the nationalist expressions of the African states. Their nationalism generally leans toward the grandiose and dreamy. It is untroubled by incompatibility of ideas, as well as tinged with reaction. Through it the African recoils from the trials of modern existence and assumes an attitude of self-admiration, self-containment, and exclusiveness. Thus African nationalism becomes a tool of disengagement in which reverberates the defiance and resentment born of present African frustrations.

In the West, Africans found institutions to be emulated, one of the most obvious being the nation-state. The achievement and maintenance of national unity and independence became the Africans' central values. African nationalists assumed the cloak of Western nationalism in their independence movements. But Western thought and values had not penetrated deeply enough to give these leaders a grasp of the principles upon which the nation-state rests. They assumed only the outward manifestations, the language and apparatus of statehood, but the real bases for unity were ignored.

The application of the standards of nationhood to an African situation where national consciousness is non-existent has been very difficult. In the African context, the dichotomy between freedom and authority has virtually necessitated the consolidation of power at the expense of individual freedom. No matter how much they are spoken of and pointed to by the African leaders, the conditions of democracy do not exist in Africa.

Hence, an agonizing process of self-accommodation was begun. In the course of this process, nationalism has been used as an apologetic device for past failures and as a defense against present difficulties, rather than as a principle of thought and action. While the process of self-accommodation has not resulted in effective political remedies, it may serve the positive purpose of deepening and broadening the Africans' understanding of the dilemmas from which their practical needs arise.

The elites of the nationalist movements are the mediators between the old and the new. They are usually products of modernization and education which have not yet touched the mass of their countrymen. They must set the ends and employ the means of modernization. Yet, the values and techniques which the elites have adopted are often inappropriate to their traditional societies.

Therefore, the new elites are strangers in their own lands, subverting the existing order and society. They quite naturally want to change it in order to satisfy their own needs. Their desire for change is in part a narrow personal wish, but is also rooted in an intense desire to bring the "better life" which they have seen elsewhere, to their countrymen. However, the amount of change needed to lead to political and cultural awakening necessarily disrupts orderly transition. The endeavor to create a united nation-state through common effort usually runs head-on into traditional patterns which strengthen factionalism and division. Such obstruction of nationalist ideals is often met by the creation of one-party states that suppress opposition and deal ruthlessly with obstructionists and factionalists.

African nationalist leaders' attitudes reflect a perceived necessity to project the undefined African image into the rest of the world. There is a strong, but dimly conceived and poorly expressed, conviction that Africa must show the world that it is unique. Part of that uniqueness is said to lie in the traditional communalism which African leaders continually emphasize. There seems to be a feeling that this communalism represents a means of co-operation that the rest of the world can and ought to learn. It is felt that the African experience, coupled with applicable modern techniques and values, will result in an internationally useful and beneficial amalgam.

On these premises rest the African nationalist convictions regarding the worth of international organization, co-operation, and continental federalism. Yet, when it comes to the practical implementation and application of these premises, Africans are generally as lost as the rest of the world, and cannot seem to find that road which will lead them to the realization of their ideals. From the negativism of anti-colonialism a great strength was drawn which made virtually an entire continent independent within a few years. But, because the time has come to replace that negativism with something positive, unity breaks down, disagreement is rampant, and progress and development are impeded. The single-minded dynamism which characterized the nationalist movements before independence is degenerating into factional quarrels and political chaos.

NOTES

1. See especially, Kwame Nkrumah, *Africa Must Unite* (New York: Frederick A. Praeger, 1963); and, *I Speak of Freedom: A Statement of African Ideology* (New York: Frederick A. Praeger, 1961).

2. Kwame Nkrumah, *Consciencism* (London: Heinemann, 1964), p. 101.

3. *Ibid.*, p. 103.

4. See especially, Gamal Abdel Nasser, *Egypt's Liberation: The Philosophy of the Revolution* (Washington, D. C.: Public Affairs

Press, 1955); and, *President Nasser's Speeches and Press Interviews* (Cairo: U.A.R. Information Service, 1963). Also, Hazem Nuseibeh, *The Ideas of Arab Nationalism* (Ithaca, N.Y.: Cornell University Press, 1957); and F. R. C. Bagley, "Nasserism," *Journal of International Affairs*, No. 2, (March, 1958).

5. For more details on Tunisia see Lorna Hahn, "North Africa: A New Pragmatism," *Orbis*, Vol. IV, No. 1 (Spring, 1964); and Charles E. Gallagher, "Bourguibism and the Tunisian Position," *American University Field Staff Reports*, Vol. III, No. 11, (1957).

6. For helpful material see, Jomo Kenyatta, *Facing Mount Kenya* (London: Acker and Warburg, 1938); and Ronald Segal, *African Profiles* (Baltimore, Md.: Penguin Books, 1963).

7. See Leopold Senghor, *African Socialism* (New York: American Society of African Culture, 1959); and *On African Socialism* (New York: Frederick A. Praeger, 1964).

8. Leopold Senghor, *African Socialism, op. cit.*, p. 12.

BIBLIOGRAPHY

APTER, DAVID E. *The Gold Coast in Transition*. Princeton, N.J.: Princeton University Press, 1955.

BRETTON, HENRY L. *Power and Stability in Nigeria*. New York: Frederick A. Praeger, 1962.

————. *The Rise and Fall of Kwame Nkrumah*. New York: Frederick A. Praeger, 1966.

COLEMAN, JAMES S. *Nigeria: Background to Nationalism*. Berkeley, Calif.: The University of California Press, 1958.

EMERSON, RUPERT and KILSON, MARTIN. *The Political Awakening of Africa*. Englewood Cliffs, N.J.: Prentice-Hall, 1965.

FERKISS, VICTOR C. *Africa's Search for Identity*. New York: George Braziller, 1966.

FRANCK, THOMAS M. *Race and Nationalism: The Struggle for Power in Rhodesia-Nyasaland*. New York: Fordham University Press, 1960.

HODGKIN, THOMAS. *Nationalism in Colonial Africa*. New York: New York University Press, 1957.

KENYATTA, JOMO. *Facing Mount Kenya*. London: Acker and Warburg, 1938.

LEWIS, I. M. *The Modern History of Somaliland: From Nation to State*. New York: Frederick A. Praeger, 1965.

LEWIS, W. ARTHUR. *Politics in West Africa.* New York: The Oxford University Press, 1965.

LISTOWEL, JUDITH. *The Making of Tanganyika.* New York: London House and Maxwell, 1966.

MACKINTOSH, JOHN P., *et al. Nigerian Government and Politics: Prelude to the Revolution.* Evanston, Ill.: Northwestern University Press, 1966.

MBOYA, TOM. *Freedom and After.* Boston: Little, Brown and Company, 1963.

ROTBERG, ROBERT I. *The Rise of Nationalism in Central Africa: The Making of Malawi and Zambia, 1873-1964.* Cambridge, Mass.: Harvard University Press, 1965.

SCHWARTZ, FREDERICK A. O., JR. *Nigeria: The Tribes, the Nation, or the Race—The Politics of Independence.* Cambridge: Massachusetts Institute of Technology Press, 1965.

SHEPPARD, GEORGE W. *The Politics of African Nationalism.* New York: Frederick A. Praeger, 1962.

WALLERSTEIN, IMMANUEL. *Africa: The Politics of Independence.* New York: Vintage Books, 1961.

ZOLBERG, ARISTOTLE R. *Creating Political Order: The Party States of West Africa.* Chicago: Rand McNally, 1966.

6 •

Progress through Socialism

Mass poverty is one of the gravest of Africa's predicaments, and the gulf between available human resources and human needs is still formidable. The lack of relevant skills and managerial talents, inordinate income differentials, irremedial pluralism, and the desire to overcome a deterministic, colonial self-image are the intertwined problems facing African leaders.

Socialism has become the a priori solution of Africa's maladies. African socialists believe that without such a generic ideology, there could be no consistent response to social needs. They assert that economic, social, and political reforms can be advanced best when African society becomes ordered by common ideological principles.

THE NATURE OF AFRICAN SOCIALISM

African socialists today believe that socialism will arise from the majority's conviction that it answers the need for a moral and just social order. The elevation of human dignity, the provision of social justice, and the equality of opportunity are foremost social values. To fulfill these, the socialists advocate the elimination of class distinction and privilege. They emphasize that this can be accomplished without violence and class warfare. Marx's assumption that capitalism necessarily leads to the impoverishment of the working class is not acceptable to them. They assume that, rather than the middle class sinking into the proletariat, the proletariat is likely to become indistinguishable from the middle class.

African socialism is an ideology as comprehensive as Africa's problems. Both African and Western socialists place particular emphasis on improving the lot of workers and peasants, but Africans give more consideration to the problems of the latter, in response to Africa's agrarian base. Both believe in democracy and individual freedom, but African socialists invoke state power more often than Western socialists because the African world is in a less advanced stage of political consolidation. Socialism in Africa is concerned primarily with agriculture, national unity, and international politics.

African socialism generally sees capital formation and accumulation as a responsibility of the government. It is possible for a centralized government agency to aid in the formation of institutions which will permit capital growth, and, at the same time, maintain careful control over the use of that capital. Governmental manipulation and planning are very much a part of the African socialist's programs, but here the African situation necessitates a degree of flexibility to make possible the most effective use of resources and capital at the same time that a socialist basis is established. The role of governments in encouraging private investment can be almost infinitely varied, as can the degree and range of governmental controls and planning.

Most of the new African states have inherited a one-crop agricultural economy from colonial days. They are actively committed to industrialization and to a reduction of continued economic dependency on a former colonizing power. Such a dependency on revenues from a fixed market leads to problems for the African socialists that must be solved pragmatically. They have a vested interest in continuing good relations with the former colonial states, to assure both continued exports and to obtain the influx of much-needed capital and trained personnel. African socialists readily accept a mixed economy which unites central planning, state operation, joint state-private enterprises, private enterprises, co-operatives, and state controls over profits and re-investment.

Virtually all African leaders are confronted with serious problems of control which are a direct result of the drive for independence and for economic and political development following independence. Foremost among these problems is gaining and maintaining strong popular support for continued economic activities that will aid in capital formation and accumulation. This must be done without creating new economic, political, and social imbalances in already precarious situations.

In the realm of control, African socialist ideology functions much as nationalism did before independence. It stresses the basic unity of the state's population and tries to imbue the whole population with the desire to work and co-operate in programs of economic development. Such popular support and unity is necessary for the establishment of socialized, independent, and industrialized states on the African continent. The people must be intimately involved, or development and stability will not follow. Of this most African socialists are firmly convinced, though the means of gaining support and involvement may vary radically from state to state.

African socialism is trying to create a will to work, sacrifice, and co-operate among all elements of the population. It is trying to transfer traditional loyalties to the larger unit of the nation-state and to mobilize energy and resources for the good of the state and its citizens. All African socialist thought has the common theme of sacrifice and work by the individual, not for selfish personal gain, but for the collective good. Here African socialism draws heavily on traditional loyalties to the clan or other kin groups, pointing out the strong collective, co-operative spirit that is seen as a characteristic of pre-colonial African society. African socialists are trying to project these traditional loyalties and experiences, and to transfer collective loyalty from the parochial kin groups to the whole nation. They are attempting to support, economically and philosophically, the nominal political changes that have already taken place in the new states of the continent.

Most African socialist thought rests on a collectivist and equalitarian self-image. African socialists assert that only in a society based on such principles can the individual find fulfillment. Such a society is seen as having a collective mind which conditions the behavior of all individuals in it. This collective mind, similar to Rousseau's concept of the general will, gives the society as a whole the right to require individual deference to the collective good. This strong assertion of egalitarianism, when united with the assertion of classlessness, defines political rights which do not flow from wealth, status, or power, but which are and must be equal for all members of society.

African socialism serves another very important purpose for the leaders of the new states. It helps to define an independent role for Africa between the East and the West. Both ideological communism and capitalism are generally discarded as inapplicable to African conditions. African socialism thus lends itself to the politics of nonalignment and speaks with an independence of mind which augurs an independence of action.

ILLUSTRATIONS OF AFRICAN SOCIALISM

Jomo Kenyatta

African socialism, as interpreted by Kenyatta, depends on uncompromising democracy.[1] It differs from communism by avowing that equal and democratic political rights must be assured for all, and from capitalism by insisting that it can and will prevent disproportionate concentration of economic and political power.

Jomo Kenyatta has spoken of African socialism as a politico-economic system which is able to, and must, borrow whatever is useful from other sources. But, in so doing, it must remain true to the basic principles of African society: it must be flexible and pragmatic to avoid the stagnation of doctrinaire positions and to meet fluid conditions; and, perhaps most important, it must not align itself internationally with any one country or bloc. Kenyatta defines African socialism as follows:

> In the phrase 'African Socialism' the word African is not introduced to describe a continent to which a foreign ideology is to be transplanted. It is meant to convey the African roots of a system that is itself African in its character, to describe an African political and economic system that is positively African

yet capable of importing useful and compatible techniques from whatever sources. The principal conditions this system must satisfy are as follows: (1) It must draw on the best of African tradition. (2) It must be adaptable to new and rapidly changing circumstances. (3) It must not rest for its success on a satellite relationship with any other country or group of countries.[2]

The ideas expressed by Kenyatta are representative of most democratic African socialists. They echo common themes which pervade the writings of Senghor and Nyerere. Yet they also share much with the more authoritarian socialism of Touré and Nkrumah.

The concept of mutual responsibility is regarded as an extension to the national level of the African family spirit, with the implied hope that this spirit may eventually be extended to an even larger community. The state, as the embodiment of the people and the popular will, is seen as having a broad obligation to provide and protect equal opportunities for its citizens, to provide social welfare services and educational facilities, to guide the economic and political development of the people, and to eliminate discrimination and exploitation.

As conceived by Kenyatta, socialism gives the leaders of the new states a vision of the future, providing them with ultimate goals to guide their pragmatic approach to immediate and pressing problems. It gives them a generalized plan of action which may be applied to everyday situations, but which must never be compromised and thereby negate the achievement of the over-all objectives.

The problems of nation-building have indicated to Kenyatta that political controls are as imperative as direct governmental intervention in the economy. He recognizes that economic activities are widely varied; to meet such diversity and to satisfy the needs of all the people, governmental programs must include a broad range of plans and controls. Such pragmatism has led Kenyatta to a virtual acceptance of the principles of a mixed economy under varying degrees of governmental supervision and control.

Kenyatta believes that mutual social responsibility conceives of the state as a means by which self-interest is harmonized with the general welfare. The assumption of social responsibility obviates the possibility of classes and class antagonisms. To assure that these clashes will not come into being, Kenyatta advocates a vigorous governmental role to prevent the concentration of economic power and speaks of the necessity for continued implementation of traditional egalitarianism.

Such an assumption leads to the immediate problem of defining how much concentration of economic resources in the hands of one group is absolutely necessary for development, and where the line must be drawn declaring such a concentration inimical to the higher interests of the society. Obviously, it is necessary to development that capital accumulation be encouraged, but Kenyatta says it must be controlled if it is not to be abused and to lead to oligarchical power.

Pragmatic acceptance of a mixed economy, when coupled with the necessity of avoiding any inordinate concentration of economic power, leads Kenyatta to promote a wide diffusion of ownership, joint ventures by the state and private investors, co-operatives, and relatively small, locally owned enterprises. State ownership, being vested in the greatest number of people, serves the double purpose of utmost diffusion of control and encouragement of genuine large-scale, mass-production techniques. Joint ventures are supported and promoted because they give the state a large measure of control over enterprise at the same time that they conserve the state's very limited capital resources by making extensive use of foreign investment capital. Guarantees are given to the foreign investors, and controls are placed on the profit and re-investment rates, to make the joint ventures as mutually beneficial as possible. It is assumed that co-operatives are rooted in African tradition and are most easily adaptable to smaller enterprises on the local, rather than the national level.

In addition, Kenyatta generally advocates progressive taxes to distribute wealth and avoid the division of classes due to wide income differentials. Such class divisions are seen as inimical to the goal of a unified society based on positive freedom for all citizens.

Leopold Senghor

One of the foremost spokesmen of African socialism is President Leopold S. Senghor of Senegal, who is often regarded as the father of democratic socialism in Africa. Senghor's main premise is that African socialism is basically a selection of those techniques for political, social, and economic development which may best be applied to African conditions.[3]

In explaining his interpretation of African socialism as a method for organizing African societies into modern states, Senghor relies heavily on Marx's concept of alienation. He sees capitalist colonialism as the vehicle by which cultural, economic, and political alienation perverted the traditional African societies. The worker was dehumanized and alienated from his production. The traditional African spirit of co-operation was submerged; selfish interests arose to create antipathy among peoples where none existed previously.

Senghor believes that the roots of communalism in traditional African social systems will make the transition to modern socialism relatively easy. He sees a social solidarity which is based on the very spirit of African life. Such solidarity was expressed before colonial days by the harmony of the individual with the collectivity of his kin group. Now it is the task of the African governments to enlarge this traditional harmony of the individual and the general interest to the scope of the nation-state, and perhaps to a confederation of African states which will emerge from a continental consciousness.

African socialism offers Senghor a means of dealing with the immediate crises of nation-building and of economic development. But, it also indicates to him a path leading to a technical and spiritual organization of society through the combination of human intelligence, love, and compassion. Such a society would offer, according to Senghor, maximum satisfaction and fulfillment for all its citizens. It would satisfy their basic human needs and achieve general well-being, democracy, and socialism.

In practical application, Senghor's socialism means training personnel, raising living and health standards, developing science and technology—in short, utilizing resources to build a distinctly African civilization. The process is, essentially, one of mental and social liberation, coupled with economic progress. Senghor sees socialism as a method of continual inquiry which aims at the betterment of man and his society.

Senghor's version of African socialism stems from the early French Utopian socialists and the scientific socialists; it has been further influenced by such later socialists as Father Pierre Teilhard de Chardin. Senghor describes the prospects of harmony in the development of a spiritual culture in almost the same breath as he speaks of the necessity for state planning and development. His is a rational, spiritual, humanist conception of the needs, desires, and capabilities of Africa.

Senghor rejects the Marxist-Leninist concept of the class struggle as inapplicable to African conditions. By assuming that Africa is already classless, he denies the necessity for violent social upheaval to build socialism, and even stresses the need of positive governmental action to avoid the creation of different classes, which would be destructive of his ends. He feels that the major goal of African socialism is not class liberation, but closing the gap between the rich and the poor states. By such a statement, he, too, casts Africa in an independent role in world affairs—the role of a go-between that might be able to harmonize relations between antagonistic blocs which threaten the existence of all.

Senghor rejects communism as it has evolved in both the Soviet Union and in China. His African socialism calls for a middle ground, on which economic development can be combined with spiritual and moral values. It is symptomatic of an African revolt against the excessive materialism of both capitalism and communism.

Practically, Senghor calls for an appraisal of the situations facing the new African states. Such an inventory would assess traditional African civilizations; the encounter between Western civilization and traditional African values, and current economic resources, needs, and potential. In his report to a party congress, Senghor stated that programs for development must not only be economic and social, but must also be culturally based. They must aim at relating the African past to the present, and project into the future.

In contrast to other African leaders, Senghor is not an advocate of one-party states. Rather, he feels that the dominant-party concept, with a strong but not alienated opposition, is best suited to African political needs. And the parties must be representative of the mass of the citizenry, for they are the central focus of political activity which can provide the substance of either cohesion or factionalism. Parties must be national and strive toward nation-building by socialization through planning and development. There is both the room and the need for differing plans and programs in order to make the democratic egalitarianism of Senghor's African socialism work.

Kwame Nkrumah

While Senghor may be representative of democratic socialism, Kwame Nkrumah is representative of a more militant and authoritarian socialism.[4] Both varieties share the common themes mentioned at the outset, but there are also some marked differences of emphasis.

Like virtually all African socialists, Nkrumah is a pragmatist who is willing and able to adapt doctrine to fit needs and conditions. Basic to Nkrumah's socialism are his conception of the political party as an elitist vanguard whose task is to move the masses towards socialism, and his conviction that society can be properly organized through the collective ownership of the means of production.

Nkrumah, like most of the socialists, relies on a conception of traditional African communalism. He assumes that socialism is the only way to give effective and modern expression to the principles which underlie that communalism. He asserts that the nature and demands of a technical society require that traditional communalism be organized and given a centralized expression through the machinery of the state. If this does not happen, class cleavages will arise and give birth to economic inequalities and political factionalism. To Nkrumah, as to Senghor, socialism is a method of applying communalism and co-operation to the needs and requirements of modern African society through eclectic borrowing:

> The restitution of Africa's humanist and egalitarian principles of society requires socialism. It is materialism that ensures the only effective transformation of nature, and socialism that desires the highest development from this transformation.[5]

Nkrumah also rejects the class-struggle doctrine of revolutionary Marxism, asserting that it is inapplicable to the predominantly classless African situation. The transition from primitive communalism to modern socialism becomes one of reform, because the basic principles of both are intrinsic to African society. Socialism is merely a reassertion of existing principles, making them appropriate to modern conditions; it is not, therefore, a revolutionary creed.

Socialism is a means of providing satisfactory material and spiritual well-being for the greatest possible number of citizens of a society. Virtually anything can be adopted to Nkrumah's flexible socialism, if it serves the interest of the whole society. Nkrumah speaks of socialism as a way of making independence meaningful and worthwhile for Africans. Independence must be expressed in a social and national context which will give the people the purpose and energy they need to build their own nations and societies.

Nkrumah has married his version of African socialism to Pan-Africanism by asserting that socialism cannot·be built effectively in just one African nation, but must be a co-operative venture. This follows from his assumption that independence for Africa is indivisible from economic independence, which can be maintained only through socialist progress and development.

Starting from these premises, Nkrumah lists the primary problems which African socialists must face in order to build socialism in their states. He avers that socialists must seek to connect the new with the old. Africa must borrow from colonialism those elements and techniques which are favorable to the interests of the people, while seeking to avoid the inequalities and antagonisms created by capitalism. The "colonial mentality" must be erased, the security and independence of the people, individually and collectively, enhanced and preserved.

Translating these ideas into practical applications, Nkrumah divides the economic life of the state into multiple sectors with the state, through its general planning and controlling agencies, exercising control over the activities in all sectors. This mixed economy includes state enterprises, co-operatives, and exclusively Ghanaian private enterprises; each sector is seen as operating within the limits set by the state. Nkrumah sees national economic planning as the principal way to all-around progress and development. Such planning must be comprehensive, ranging from large-scale industrial and public works projects to the smallest village co-operative. It must unite general economic development with education, welfare, and health programs. It must also be flexible enough to allow for adjustments, so that when contingencies arise the economic balance will not be thrown off.

Planners must devote a good portion of their time to controlling the re-investment of private capital profits, domestic and foreign. Nkrumah justifies this by asserting that the states in which the profits are made should receive a generous proportion of the benefits derived. Likewise, guarantees of a basic minimum standard of living for all the population should be an integral part of the planning operation. Popular participation in the planning process should be encouraged through political organizations and voluntary associations which help to mobilize support for the government's program.

Nkrumah is authoritarian insofar as he believes in the necessity of a one-party state, insists on strict party discipline within the elite group, and outlaws opposition to party programs and policies once they have been instituted. Since 1960, and until his overthrow on February 24, 1966, Nkrumah fostered a cult around himself not only as a leader of Ghanaian development and socialism, but also as the potential leader of a Pan-African union which would dutifully follow the doctrines of Nkrumaism. His faith does not lie so much in the mass of the population and in popular democracy as it does in the "principles of communalism" in socialist planning and in the vanguard party which he believes can build a new African continental society.

Gamal Abdel Nasser

The Arab socialist movement had its origins in Western socialist thought as well as in the Islamic legacy.[6] Some reform movements sought to improve Arab society through a return to traditional Islam; others, through the adoption of radical Westernization; while a more moderate school of thought attempted to find the means of reform both in the tenets of the past and in the revolutionary ideology of the modern world.

Arab socialism was stamped by the circumstances surrounding the Arab struggles for self-determination and independence. Their historical experience has transmitted to the Arabs a legacy of political insecurity and a desire for progress and security. To many Arabs, socialism is the ideology which best corresponds to their needs and promises the fulfillment of their aspirations. They feel that the nationalist and socialist movements complement each other, and that socialism should constantly be adapted to meet the changing needs and interests of Arab society. Above all, they believe that socialism should serve the national purpose.

Socialist parties were not formed in the nineteenth century when the need for social and economic reforms was most urgent. This delay can be attributed to the Arab preoccupation with achieving independence. In the early twentieth century there appeared some vague references to socialism by reformers, and some minor movements called for its adoption (such as the short-lived *Al-Hizb al-Ishtiraki Al Mubarak,* The Blessed Socialist Party, organized by Muhammad Jamal al-Din in 1908, in Egypt). In the inter-war period, however, socialist parties were organized in several Arab states, for example, *Misr al-Fatat** (Young Egypt) in 1933 in Egypt and *al-Baath* (The Arab Resurrection Party) in 1941 in Syria. They sought to achieve economic democracy by replacing the feudal and capitalist system with a socialist system in which the interests of the community would have priority over individual claims.

Following the attainment of independence, particularly in the late fifties, socialism began to gain influence in the Arab states. The Arab socialists sought to reform their societies by introducing modern scientific measures, adopting Western methods that fit the needs of the Arab states, and preserving those parts of the Arab legacy and heritage that offer positive contributions to development and progress. However, they realized that they needed an independent and stable society in order to implement these reforms. They were concerned not only with socialism, but also with the general formulation of Arab national and international policy. Socialists were among the original proponents of positive neutralism for the Arab world, and they have been influential in bringing about the adoption of that policy by African governments.

Like most African socialists, President Nasser of Egypt has moved toward socialism according to the dictates of political and economic conditions in his country.[7] Between the 1952 coup d'état and the 1955 Bandung Conference, socialism was not part of his main concern. He was primarily anti-imperialistic— he wanted to emancipate the peasants; he was not greatly interested in building a socialist state. But, by organizing co-operatives to meet more effectively the economic demands of his country, he began to move gradually along a road that eventually led him to a socialist posture.

Bandung brought Nasser into a world of socialist neutralism. He was impressed by the potentials of the neutralist bloc, by socialist development schemes, and by the Chinese revolution. He was determined that Egypt should have a major role to play.

*Renamed Socialist Democratic Party in 1946.

When his pet project, the Aswan Dam, was threatened by withdrawal of Western aid, he turned decisively to socialism as a means of meeting the financial crisis.

Many of Nasser's socialist ideas are the result of his strong personal friendship with, and admiration for, Marshal Tito of Yugoslavia. The co-operative schemes, mixed economy, and planning and control agencies which he has sought to introduce into Egypt are patterned after the Yugoslav model.

To offset the loss of Western funds, Nasser nationalized the Suez Canal in June, 1956. Egyptian management struggled through, and within a few years revenues were steadily increasing. This was Nasser's first experiment with nationalization, and it proved to him what could be done, given the right personnel and conditions.

By the time Nasser had successfully negotiated a loan for Aswan with the U.S.S.R. in 1960, he was firmly espousing a socialist position. In July, 1961, Nasser issued a series of decrees asserting government control of major industrial and financial interests. Railroads, transports, foreign trade, and textile industries were nationalized, while controlling interests were obtained in hundreds of other enterprises. At the same time, taxes were made progressive and were increased, income limits were set, minimum wage laws were passed, profits were divided among welfare programs, and workers' councils were established to aid in business operation.

Nasser's Arab socialism, as espoused in the Arab Socialist Union, is openly associated with Islam and rejects the dictatorship of the proletariat and nationalization of land. He exploits certain capitalist elements as means of aiding the development of socialism in Egypt. He does not accept the class-struggle doctrine of orthodox Marxist-Leninist thought.

Nasser's socialist planning is based on a mixed economy, but with dominant power in public hands. It envisions a public sector comprising 80 per cent of the economy and strictly controlling the subservient private sector. One target of planning is to double the national income every decade—population control is linked to this goal. Land holdings will remain private, but are to be limited. Irrigation and drainage are public services, and co-operatives are to be further expanded. Trade unionism is joined to the socialist development of industry. Foreign aid and investment are sought, but must be without any stipulations and are described officially as taxes on the former colonial imperialists.

Nasser is trying to unite his concept of Arab socialism to a popular democracy. He wants to arouse popular dynamic support which can later be developed into at least quasi-democratic constitutionalism. However, the U.A.R. is still a one-party state; Nasser is as yet reluctant to trust the will of an illiterate peasantry which he feels is still unfit for the tasks of popular government.

Just as African socialism is linked with Pan-Africanism by the socialists of sub-Saharan Africa, so Nasser connects his brand of socialism with Pan-Arabism. He sees Pan-Arabism as uniting the Arab countries from Morocco to Iraq and enabling them to play a major role in world politics through the neutral bloc.

Habib Bourguiba

An alternative to Nasser's socialism is found in Tunisia. Bourguiba's Destourian (Constitutional) socialism would seem to have great substantive affinity with the socialism of Nasser.[8] Nonetheless, appeals to Pan-Arabism are conspicuously absent in Tunisia. Bourguiba emphasizes pragmatic planning by state authorities rather than rigid control. He also calls upon the individual citizen to play a part in the orientation of planning; however, such participation, is to be channelled through party cells and party-controlled trade unions. But in trying to strike a mean course between individual initiative and governmental control, Destourian socialism faces a paradox.

Economic and social underdevelopment and a mass mentality of stagnation are mutually reinforcing factors. Consequently, Bourguiba's pleas for public discipline fall upon deaf ears. Bourguiba realizes that a precondition of socialism is the psychological transformation of the Tunisian people. Claiming to draw inspiration from the traditional Islamic concept of community, he wants to instill the mentality of social responsibility in his people.

THE PROSPECTS FOR AFRICAN SOCIALISM

Although there is no single body of African socialist doctrine, several themes are common to all variations. African socialists are concerned primarily with the problem of a continental African identity and the struggle to emerge from underdevelopment into modernization.

The search for a continental (and essentially Negro) identity is linked to the desire of African leaders to develop an ideology which will guide their political actions, unite their states by providing a solid basis for development, and assert African independence of action in a world torn between giant powers. Such an ideology must reject what to the Africans are the most odious influences from the colonial past.

African socialists imagine that there is a solid basis for socialism in the traditional social system of their countries. The traditional communalism is seen as the root for the development of a socialist system on which African society will be organized to meet the needs and challenges of independence and development. Socialism is declared to be "natural" to Africa. Capitalism, on the other hand, is foreign to these traditions, primarily because of its emphasis on individualism and competition rather than on co-operation.

Great emphasis is placed on the problem of economic development. Virtually all African socialists draw a correlation between economic development and an extensive role for government. There are, however, no commonly accepted rigid formulae. A fluidity in economic policy formulation has led to an active search for private investment capital which may be used effectively in a mixed economy. But it is clear that the role of the African governments will be greater in economic development than has been the case with many industrializing states which relied on the private sector.

Among African socialists there is a general distrust of the entrepreneurial class, which is seen as being self-interested rather than contributing to the general welfare of the nation. This leads to an unfavorable attitude toward the development of an independent African bourgeoisie. Because of this, most governments are encouraging co-operative ventures to a greater degree than private enterprise. Yet, at the same time that the African socialists are generally inhibiting the growth of a native bourgeoisie, they are actively searching for foreign private capital that can be invested to aid internal development. Such importation of foreign capital serves the double purpose of financing programs and of preventing local groups from gaining inordinate economic power that could be turned later into political power.

It is important to point out here that while many people in the West do not make a distinction between revolutionary Marxism as a means of progress and development and Marxism as an ideology, Africans and non-Westerners do. It is essential that we understand the basis of this distinction and the reasons for making it.

The peoples of Asia and Africa are, if we delve beneath their rhetoric, committed to the civilization of the Western world. They attempt—whether consciously or unconsciously—to fit the accomplishments of that civilization into the framework of their own states. However, with regard to a philosophy of change and development, the non-West has turned to other sources for inspiration and direction.

Until the Russian Revolution in 1917, states which sought to modernize and industrialize had available to them only one comprehensive blueprint for progress: nineteenth-century capitalism. The Bolshevik Revolution of 1917, however, brought with it an alternative pattern for change—socialism or communism.

The new states of the non-West have before them the success story of a communist society. They can point—with some justification—to the progress of the Soviet Union over the past decades and can conclude that, were it not for their socialistic or communistic theory, the extensive development which the Soviets have achieved would not have occurred. Of course, in saying that Russia in 1917 was a totally backward, agrarian, peasant state, the non-Western states neglect embarrassing facts. Pre-Bolshevik Russia had already constructed a partial infrastructure for modernization. Nonetheless, the Soviet experiment has certainly impressed the states of the non-West.

Impatient to achieve their goals and to realize progress, oblivious to the phenomenon of twentieth-century welfare capitalism, the non-West has rejected a considerable portion of the Western pattern of development. Unwilling to follow painstakingly this centuries-long blueprint for progress, the non-West favors "socialism": the centralization of power and authority, government intervention in, or control of, industrialization, economic planning, and the like.

It should be understood that the non-Western states have not adopted purely "Soviet" or "communistic" models. They are reshaping these models to fit their own unique frameworks, traditions, and modes of life. They are seeking to adopt the relevant and the desirable so as to achieve their own ends and goals in their own fashion. They are borrowing from both East and West—revising and readjusting in order to meet their own needs. Impatience, the desire for rapid development, the lack of agreed-upon criteria, and the search for dignity and status account for many of these contradictory choices and decisions. However, it is doubtful that the Africans could reconcile liberalism as a way of life and revolutionary Marxism as a process of change. At the present stage of African history, liberalism has been sacrificed on the altar of nation-building. This is understandable. The future of Africa will be determined by the ability of its leaders to strike a mean course.

NOTES

1. See "African Socialism and Its Relation to Planning In Kenya," a pamphlet published by the Kenya Government in 1965. Also, Jomo Kenyatta, *Facing Mount Kenya* (London: Acker and Warburg, 1938) for his early views of the problem of development.

2. *African Forum: A Quarterly Journal of African Affairs,* I, No. 1, (1965), p. 26.

3. See Leopold S. Senghor, *African Socialism* (New York: American Society of African Culture, 1959); and *On African Socialism* (New York: Frederick A. Praeger, 1964).

4. See Kwame Nkrumah, *Ghana: The Autobiography of Kwame Nkrumah* (New York: Thomas Nelson, 1957); and *I Speak of Freedom: A Statement of African Ideology* (New York: Frederick A. Praeger, 1961).

5. Kwame Nkrumah, *Consciencism* (London: Heinemann, 1964), p. 77.

6. See Hazem Zaki Nuseibeh, *The Ideas of Arab Nationalism* (Ithaca: The Cornell University Press, 1956); Mizra M. Husain, *Islam and Socialism* (Lahore: Muhammad Ashraf, 1947); John Hardie (trans.), Sayed Kotb's *Social Justice in Islam* (Ann Arbor: Edwards Brothers, 1953).

7. For further study see H. L. Hoskins, "Arab Socialism in the U.A.R.," *Current History,* January, 1963.

8. For a study of Bourguiba see C. H. Moore, "Bourguibism in Tunisia," *Current History,* January, 1963.

BIBLIOGRAPHY

"African Socialism and Its Relation to Planning in Kenya," a Republic of Kenya pamphlet, 1965.

BATTEN, T. R. *Problems of African Development.* (3rd ed.), London: Oxford University Press, 1960.

BROCKWAY, A. FENNER. *African Socialism.* London: The Bodley Head, Ltd., 1963.

DUMONT, RENE. *False Start in Africa.* New York: Frederick A. Praeger, 1966.

FRIEDLAND, WILLIAM H. and ROSBERG, CARL J., JR. *African Socialism.* Stanford, Calif.: Stanford University Press, 1964.

HUSAIN, MIZRA M. *Islam and Socialism.* Lahore: Muhammad Ashraf, 1947.

O'BRIEN, PATRICK. *The Revolution in Egypt's Economic System: From Private Enterprise to Socialism, 1952-65.* New York: The Oxford University Press, 1966.

SENGHOR, LEOPOLD. *African Socialism.* New York: American Society of African Culture, 1959.

————. *On African Socialism.* New York: Frederick A. Praeger, 1964.

7 ◆

Order through Pan-Africanism

A trend discernible in the rhetoric of contemporary African nation-building is that all African leaders, while striving for national unification, generally subscribe to the broader goal of Pan-Africanism. It is no surprise, however, that although these leaders arrive at a consensus regarding ends there is wide disagreement over the means of attaining them.

The appeals of Pan-Africanism are numerous. Negatively, Pan-Africanism is a response to the social, political, and economic alienation which resulted from the colonial experience. Positively, Pan-Africanism rests upon the assumption that all Africans share a common heritage. The conviction that Africans have been more oppressed, exploited, and degraded than any other group of peoples is the spiritual and moral foundation of the African drive for unity and co-operation. Its realization involves the creation of an African commonwealth, a political organization of united African states.

Were continental unity to be achieved, such radical Pan-Africanists as Nkrumah argue, Africa could attain full political and cultural equality in the world, compete on equal terms in the international system, and remain aloof from the political machinations of non-African powers. For unity is strength, and continental harmony would further the attainment of positive freedom and equality.

But on realistic grounds, the assumption that a common heritage provides an adequate basis for unity is open to debate. In the current African political scene, the desperate struggle to insure minimal order within each national framework appears to discourage movements for unification on a more grandiose scale.

The sentiments of Pan-Africanism have played a role in consolidating states. They have furnished tools to undergird national integration, to legitimize power, to create traditions, and have provided a pattern for modernizing without westernizing. This attempt to break down the reality of western superiority serves to build up the Africans' confidence in their own ability to create viable political institutions.

Pan-Africanism is perhaps the clearest example of the process by which African leaders hope to develop an African philosophy and view of the world. It is a source of both instrumental and substantive values. As an ideology, it serves as a conceptual basis for day-to-day policy-making. However, it is as a Utopia that Pan-Africanism has gained widespread appeal.

Pan-Africanism seeks to revive the African mystique of unity and brotherhood. From the colonial experience and the infusion of Western values and ideals there has also emerged a concept of *negritude*, a racial consciousness and pride based on what is interpreted as the traditional African quality of compassion. Compassion distinguished African man; it is the basis of African communal co-operation; it provides African nationalists with an easy means of identification with the African past. There is a passionate longing to obtain what was denied Africa under colonialism: to prove that Africa has a will, character, and a soul of its own.

Africans further imagine that the moderating force of Pan-Africanism will aid greater international co-operation. That is, a united Africa could both play the role of mediator in international conflicts and serve as a bridge between West and non-West, East and West. Pan-Africanism has all the characteristics of a renaissance designed to combine the "greatness" of a dim past with a new-found sense of international political status. Thus, Africans feel that their struggle will not be concluded until continental and perhaps global unity is achieved. Whether these passions and ideals are strong enough to support the practical application of Pan-Africanism is open to serious question. Will the ideals of a Pan-African union of free states survive the rigorous demands of the African political environment—or the reassertion of African rivalries? The possibilities of channelling such deep political emotions into competing nationalisms are just as great and as numerous as the forces which originally led to the development of the Pan-African sentiment itself. And to the African masses and their leaders, faced with the pressing problems of development and material progress, these more parochial ties may have greater immediate and pragmatic relevance.

EVOLUTION OF PAN-AFRICANISM

Pan-Africanism can best be understood in the light of its historical development. During its initial stage of growth, between 1918 and 1958, it served as a protest movement against western cultural dominance and a rallying point which gave impetus to the drive for independence. Currently, it represents independent Africa's search for an African form of community and order within the international system.

Origins

The concept of Pan-Africanism arose from a conglomeration of ideals uniting Africans and the peoples of African descent. Henry Sylvester-Williams, a West Indian lawyer, found himself in sympathy with the several West Africans whom he encountered in London. He later acted as legal advisor to a political mission of African tribal chiefs. In 1900, he organized an African Conference in London. The conference served as a forum of protest against white colonialism and generated an appeal to British missionaries and abolitionists for assistance in a struggle for total African independence.

The African Conference of 1900 attracted wide attention. Queen Victoria responded by promising not to "overlook the interests and welfare of the native races." But Sylvester-Williams died a few years afterwards, and Pan-Africanism went into decline until after World War I.

The movement was revived by W. E. B. Du Bois, an American Negro historian—and a Marxist—who organized five international Pan-African congresses between 1919 and 1945. Du Bois was in Paris in 1918, hoping to persuade the victorious Allied Powers to adopt a Charter of Human Rights for Africans to compensate for services of African Negroes on the Western front. He was assisted in his efforts by a Senegalese Negro Deputy to the French Assembly, Blaise-Diagne, who, as *commissaire-générale* for West Africa, had recruited nearly a million soldiers and laborers during the war. With permission obtained by Diagne from Prime Minister Clemenceau, the first Pan-African Congress was held in Paris while the peace negotiations were still in progress.

The first Congress unanimously adopted a petition requesting that the Allied Powers place the former German African colonies of Togoland, Cameroons, Southwest Africa, and Tanganyika under international supervision until they could become self-governing. The Congress also adopted a resolution embodying three principal demands: (1) that the Allied and Associated Powers codify laws similar to the proposed international labor code, for the protection of the natives of Africa; (2) that the League of Nations establish a permanent bureau to promote the political, social, and economic welfare of the natives; (3) that the existing African colonial governments be converted to protective trusteeships. The resolution also urged a higher regard for African social needs, the regulation of investment capital, restraints on the exploitation and exhaustion of natural resources, the abolition of slavery and corporal punishment, state regulation of labor, public education, and finally, the participation of native Africans in the colonial governments.

The second Pan-African Congress held its first session in London in 1921, met in Brussels for its second session, and finished its work in Paris. The Congress restated its demands for colonial reforms and recommended to the Mandates Commission of the League of Nations that, in view of the growing African desire for self-government, Negroes be appointed to the Commission. Du Bois attempted to establish a permanent Pan-African secretariat to maintain contacts between the representatives, but was unable to carry out his organization plans until the fifth Pan-African Congress.

The third Pan-African Congress met in London and Lisbon in 1923, and the fourth met in New York in 1927. In the following years, Negroes throughout the world were especially hard hit by the Great Depression and the next Congress was repeatedly postponed. But nonetheless, the Pan-African movement did its most constructive work in the depression years. The fourth Congress had found it necessary to defend its program against both the proponents of the status quo and the challenge of Communist opportunism. In the spirit of the fourth Congress, many African intellectuals undertook selective studies of European political theories and systems. Their studies were eventually consolidated in a nationalist program for the application of Western political methods to traditional African organizations.

During World War II, articles on Pan-Africanism began to appear in West African newspapers. Nnamdi Azikiwe (President of Nigeria, 1963-66), the leader of the National Council of Nigeria and the Cameroons (NCNC), published a polemical article on self-determination entitled, "The Atlantic Charter and British West Africa." He suggested the formation of transnational governments which would eventually provide for self-government of the British West African territories within the British Commonwealth. Also during the war years, the Pan-African Federation was formed in the United Kingdom to organize a united front of Negro political, labor, religious, educational, and social organizations.

The fifth Pan-African Congress, held in England in 1945, was distinctly different from the four preceding it. While earlier congresses were attended mainly by intellectuals, the fifth congress attracted trade unionists, workers, and students. The resolutions of this conference asserted that the rights of the peoples of Africa were being violated by the imperialist powers and that the principles of the Four Freedoms and the Atlantic Charter should be implemented.

Messages were sent to peoples and governments around the world, encouraging them in their struggles to break with colonialism. The Congress appealed for a more militant approach to problems affecting Africa and peoples of African descent throughout the world.

The fifth Congress adopted a program of non-violent non-co-operation based upon Gandhian principles. In 1950, this program was utilized effectively in the Gold Coast (Ghana) by Kwame Nkrumah. Thus, Pan-Africanism entered a phase of positive action, the effectiveness of which depended upon the ability of the African peoples to organize. In the action phase, the task of leadership fell largely upon the nationalists, for the intellectuals lacked the active support of the common people. Widespread political action began in 1947, when the NCNC sent a delegation to London to protest the provisions of the 1945 constitution which had been imposed on Nigeria. In 1948 and again in 1950, Nkrumah and other elected leaders of the Gold Coast Trade Union Congress and Convention Peoples' Party (CPP) were imprisoned. However, Nkrumah's star kept rising, and together with the CPP candidates he was elected for the Accra Central in the 1951 election, while still in jail. This was a definite victory for the Pan-African cause. Nkrumah's political rivals, the conservative tribal chiefs, failed in their attempts to label the CPP as a dangerous Communist threat, and Nkrumah was able to reaffirm his intention of linking his West African Federation to the broader Pan-African movement.

Emergence of Pan-African Groupings

When Pan-Africanism returned to Africa in 1958, after virtual exile in Europe and America, it rested on broad and ill-defined programs of action for nationalist groups. These programs were based on the following general principles:

(1) "Africa for Africans:" an expression of anti-colonialism implying independence from all forms of foreign involvement in the African continent.

(2) African federalism: a vague ideal conceptualizing the ultimate creation of a single, continental African state.

(3) The African Personality: the reassertion of the unique African essence in culture, politics, economic development, and the arts.

(4) A new communalism: the creation of viable, integrated communities to replace traditional tribalism, together with the creation of a continental African loyalty which would transcend the particularistic nationalism of the new states.

(5) African socialism: the combination of traditional communalistic practices with modern techniques in the interest of economic development and material well-being.

(6) A belief in democracy as the best and most appropriate form of political organization for the African societies.

(7) Gandhi's non-violence coupled with Nkrumah's positive action as a means toward independence for all of Africa.

(8) Non-alignment with either cold war power bloc, and the vigorous assertion of a concerted African effort in international affairs.

As the Pan-African movement grew, and new voices were added to the chorus, some placed primary emphasis on certain of these factors, and some on others. A variety of means for the achievement of African unity and a variety of interpretations of the nature of that unity were put forward as each Pan-African leader devised a personal solution to the problem.

A new phase in the development of Pan-Africanism began with Nkrumah's assumption of the dominant role among African nationalists. The two conferences in Accra, in April and December of 1958, gave new form and direction to the Pan-African movement: Nkrumah put his stamp of "federalism through positive action" on both meetings.[1]

The April Conference of the Eight Independent States of Africa aimed at promoting friendship, co-operation, brotherhood, and solidarity among the new states and the nationalist groups working for independence in the colonial areas. Though the tone of the conference was anti-colonial, it was quite moderate in its demands; no specific reference was made to the goal of African union. The conference was the first to voice the concept of "African personality," and it was agreed that this concept could and should serve as a unifying symbol of the aspirations of all Africa. African members of the United Nations were urged to co-ordinate their policies whenever possible. Machinery for this task was not set up immediately, but the groundwork was laid for the December conference.

The December All-African Peoples Conference met to discuss the problems and prospects of Pan-Africanism. It was made plain that the ultimate goal of Pan-Africanism was federation of the entire continent. But Nkrumah clearly showed his federalist bias by successfully promoting his program of unity through federalism. It was decided that the movement's immediate objective would be the creation of regional federations which would serve as steppingstones to eventual continental unity.

The voice of another nationalist leader made itself heard at the second Accra conference: that of Kenya's Tom Mboya. He argued that, despite the Pan-African tradition of non-violent

civil disobedience, it was the right and duty of Africans everywhere to bend the means to fit the situation and to strike force-
fully, if necessary, when independence was at stake. If violence
was used to suppress Africans, counter-violence was the appropriate response.

Other concerns of the second Accra conference were the
necessity for modernization and tribal obstruction of freedom
and development. The latter issue, however, was not a blanket
condemnation of the African past. It was, instead, an attempt
to synthesize the best of the old and new African values. As a
means to its chosen goals, the Accra conference recommended
active government participation in the integration and modernization process. A moderate socialist spirit was evident in the
proposals and declarations on economic integration of national
and regional economies.

The creation of the All-African Peoples Organization
(AAPO) was stimulated by the Accra conference of December,
1958. As a non-official organization of African political parties,
it did not speak for governments; however, it did serve as a useful
forum for the discussion of African problems. Led by Nkrumah,
the AAPO explored the implications of federalism in Africa. It
pledged itself to the support of nationalist groups in those territories where democratic processes were not available as a means
of gaining independence, but reiterated its preference for a
non-violent approach. At successive conferences in Tunis and
Cairo, the AAPO upheld these positions and re-emphasized the
non-racial character of the Pan-African movement. The AAPO
asserted that its goal was the ultimate creation of a multi-racial,
federal African continental state based on mass democracy and
committed to socialist development. It relied heavily on Nkrumah's ideology and the experience of his program in Ghana.

Nkrumah was unable to maintain his personal leadership of
the Pan-African and the united liberation movements for long
after the Accra conferences. The independence of Nigeria and
thirteen former French colonies in 1960 contributed to his
decline. Various divergent schemes were posed as challenges to
his federalist-socialist approach. Even though Guinea joined
Ghana in a nominal union in 1958, when Nkrumah and Touré
met in 1959 to discuss the formation of a Community of
Independent African States, nothing substantive was actually
accomplished.

Meanwhile, in the French-African community, Senegal and Sudan established the Mali Federation of 1959. The Ivory Coast, Upper Volta, and Dahomey refused to participate however, and under the leadership of Felix Houphouet-Boigny, they joined with Niger in a loose economic organization, the *Conseil de l'Entente*. The *Conseil de l'Entente* provided for a customs union, a common communications system, and a joint judicial system. The *Entente* envisioned the gradual regulation of all inter-governmental affairs and the co-ordination of the domestic and foreign policies of its members. But, because of Houphouet-Boigny's caution and understandable reluctance to redistribute the comparative wealth of the Ivory Coast among the less-developed members, the unity of the *Entente* remained tenuous.

Another group, the Union of African and Malagasy States, otherwise known as the UAMS, was conceived at a meeting in the Ivory Coast in October, 1960. The following November, a full-scale conference was held at Brazzaville,[2] where it was decided to form a more permanent association of the twelve former French colonial states. The UAMS met again at Yaoundé in March, 1961 to formulate unified policies. It was able to develop co-operation in defense and foreign policies and an Afro-Malagasy Economic Cooperation Organization (AMEC) envisaging common economic institutions. In 1962, the organization devised plans for a joint shipping and airline company, and a unified policy towards the United Nations and the European Economic Community (EEC).

In spite of a genuine desire for eventual federation and the obvious necessity of development and defense co-operation, factional rivalries destroyed the Mali federation in August, 1960. Mali, formerly the French Sudan, later joined Ghana and Guinea in a new Union of African States (UAS), in 1960. This organiza-tion was based on Nkrumah's vision of continental federation, but was unable to proceed beyond occasional consultations and formalistic ministerial meetings.

The Ghana-Guinea-Mali Union of African States failed to produce effective political institutions. It served, rather, as a sounding board for the assertions of Nkrumah and Touré that federation was both immediately necessary and feasible. The primary result of the continued existence of the UAS was the increasing isolation of its three members from the other less mili-tant, more gradualist and functionalist UAMS group.

Partially as a response to the successes of the UAMS and the inefficiency of the UAS, five states—Ghana, Guinea, Mali, Morocco, the UAR—and representatives from Libya and Algeria's National Liberation Front (FLN) met in Casablanca at the invitation of King Mohammed V of Morocco, in January, 1961. The King's immediate motives for convening the conference centered around the situation in the Congo and his failure to win support in the United Nations for Morocco's claims to Mauritania.

The Casablanca Conference provided for the establishment of the African Consultative Assembly. This Assembly was to meet periodically "with a view to ensuring the common defense of Africa in the case of aggression and to safeguard the independence of African states."[4] The Assembly has never met, although to the outside world this conference appeared to signify a great unifying step forward. However, skeptics quickly pointed out that it could hardly be representative because so few states had participated.

The five Casablanca powers met again at Conakry in July, 1961; there they outlined plans for the progressive establishment of a customs union. They also discussed the organization of a Permanent Council in African Unity and a Central Bank for African Development. They proposed the establishment of an All-African Trade Union Federation as a step towards Pan-African union. They demanded that other African states sever relations with the "western dominated" International Confederation of Trade Unions.

The divergent approaches of the federalist UAS and the more moderate and definitely functionalist UAMS led to the Monrovia Conference of May, 1961.[5] Presidents Tubman, Senghor, and Olympio joined with Premier Balewa in calling a twenty-state conference to settle the growing differences between the two regional blocs.

The Monrovia Conference took the same militant view toward colonialism as did the AAPO and the UAS, but compromised between the positions of the Casablanca and Brazzaville groups. For the first time, Nigeria's Balewa asserted his leadership. He guided the Conference toward a firm stand which favored increased economic and political co-operation, but also emphasized the necessity of maintaining complete national sovereignty. This was an attempt to reach a compromise between the UAS and the UAMS positions, but it did not totally succeed in reconciling the two factions.

The Conference expressed regret that the UAS states had not chosen to attend the Monrovia Conference, but hoped that they would join in future meetings to be held in Lagos to discuss the implementation of joint development programs. However, the moderate tone of the conference so incensed the UAS powers that a violent split occurred, with press attacks flying from both sides.

The Monrovia Declaration set the basic guidelines which were reaffirmed in the Lagos Conference of January, 1962, and were later followed at the Addis Ababa Conference of the Organization of African Unity (OAU) in 1963. African co-operation and development were to be achieved by faithful adherence to five basic principles: (1) equality and sovereignty of states; (2) territorial integrity of states; (3) freedom of regional organization; (4) non-interference in internal affairs of other states; (5) condemnation of subversion from whatever source.

In contrast to the UAS-Casablanca group, the Monrovia bloc committed itself to co-operation in the gradual functional organization of African economies, as well as in the gradual development of political co-operation. At Monrovia, the majority of African states stressed their common concern with the preservation of national sovereignty, warily side-stepping Nkrumah's proposals for immediate and complete federation of the continent.

Still another group of African states, sponsored by Julius Nyerere, met in 1962 to discuss the possibilities of federation in East and Central Africa. The Pan-African Freedom Movement for East, Central, and South Africa (PAFMECSA) included representatives from Tanganyika, Zanzibar, Uganda, Kenya, Ruanda-Burundi, Nyasaland, the Rhodesias, Somalia, and Ethiopia, as well as nationalist groups from South Africa, Southwest Africa, Bechuanaland, Basutoland, and Swaziland.

PAFMECSA is an outgrowth of extremely loose groupings of political parties under the general leadership of Jomo Kenyatta, Julius Nyerere, and Tom Mboya. According to it regional, political, and economic organizations, and continental economic co-operation should precede African political federation.

PAFMECSA is formally committed, however, to the establishment of a future East African central government. So far, it has failed to create a substructure on which to build these grandiose ideals.

If PAFMECSA has enjoyed little success in co-ordinating immediate political and economic policies, and in implementing its broader goals for the future, the East African Common Services Organization (EACSO), more specialized in function and limited in membership, offers a greater promise for closing the gap between African expectations and accomplishments. The precedent for East African regionalism was established under colonialism. In 1938 the East African High Commission came into being to furnish a joint approach to the social, economic, and political problems of the colonies of Kenya, Uganda, and Tanganyika (now Tanzania).

The Commission's functions were assumed after independence by EACSO, which was formed in 1961. In many ways, EACSO could serve as a model for African regionalism: the integrative approach used in meeting many common problems has been functional, and, at the same time, it has forced a greater political dialogue, if not political agreement, between the three governments.

EACSO received a substantial shot in the arm on June 6, 1967, when the East African Cooperation Treaty was signed by Presidents Kenyatta, Nyerere and Obote. One of the most outstanding features of the present treaty is the provision for correcting trade imbalances. The treaty specifies that a state which is in deficit in its total trade in manufactured goods with the other two states may impose transfer taxes upon goods equivalent in value to its deficit with those countries. In the future, the provisions for a properly regulated system of transfer taxes will work towards levelling off trade between states and ensuring that the advantages of co-operation are shared equitably.

Another outstanding feature of the treaty is the establishment of the East African Development Bank. First of all, it recognizes the existence of an economic community rather than autarchic markets. Additionally, it acknowledges that within the community there are poorer and richer areas. There will be a guarantee that no parts of the community will remain in the backwash of the community's general prosperity.

THE ORGANIZATION OF AFRICAN UNITY (OAU)

The heads of state and representatives from thirty-two states both north and south of the Sahara met at Addis Ababa in May, 1963, to form the Organization of African Unity. That year was hailed as the year of Africa's rebirth as a unified continent, for it seemed that at least some semblance of true unity would be achieved.

Nkrumah attempted to impose his federalist position on the group by intensive lobbying and propaganda activities, but met with little enthusiasm and less success. The resulting organization reflected the more moderate proposals of the Monrovia group.

According to the OAU charter, the organization is committed:

> (1) to promote the unity and solidarity of the African states; (2) to coordinate and intensify their cooperation and efforts to achieve a better life for the peoples of Africa; (3) to defend their sovereignty, their integrity, and independence; (4) to eradicate all forms of colonialism from Africa; (5) to promote international cooperation, having due regard to the Charter of the United Nations and the Universal Declaration of Human Rights.[6]

The OAU called upon each of its members to co-ordinate their policies in the fields of domestic and foreign affairs, economic development, educational and cultural advancement, social welfare services, scientific and technical development, and defense and security. The OAU charter reflects the basic Pan-African principles of socialism, anticolonialism, racial equality, neutralism, non-violence, and restricted federalism. It set up an organizational structure designed to overcome regional factionalism and, at the same time, encourage regional co-operation.

Perhaps most importantly, the OAU charter emphasizes the desire of virtually all the African states to speak with a concerted voice in international politics. The OAU is at least a partial expression of that desire and represents a first step toward the development of a specifically African presence in world affairs.

Following the formation of the Organization of African Unity in May, 1963, the contrasts and divisive forces between the UAS and the Monrovia group were markedly diminished. As a result, the first OAU foreign ministers' conference was held at Dakar in August, 1963, to discuss the orderly dismantling of African regional groups. Simultaneously, however, the UAMS met to determine ways in which it could continue to co-operate with the OAU while retaining the functions and organizational structure of the UAMS. The UAMS states voted to co-operate with the OAU and to participate fully in the OAU labor organization. In this way it would be possible for the UAMS to realize immediate benefits from the functional aspect of the OAU regional arrangement, and still be assured of future benefits should the OAU prove to be a total success. PAFMECSA has taken a similar position, choosing to concentrate on regional problems until the continental organization proves itself.

Since its formation in 1963, the OAU has expanded to include all independent African states, excluding Rhodesia and the Republic of South Africa. It is looked upon as a means of strengthening each of the individual member states through co-operative action and co-ordination of policies. Virtually all its members concur in its procedural method: a functional, pragmatic approach to immediate problems, and the continued pursuit of a long-range goal of political federation. Whether or not the federalist aim is achieved, its pursuit will satisfy a basic requirement of the Pan-African ideal, and the immediate benefits of a functional approach will be realized.

For the present, the Organization of African Unity serves only to reveal existing differences and approaches to the problem of nation-building. It has momentarily reconciled the moderate and radical approaches to the problem of community at the national, regional, and international levels in a way that reflects the basic divisions that have separated Africa along ideological and political lines since the onset of independence.

It is possible to divide the OAU analytically into radical and moderate sectors. The radical nationalists identify militant Pan-Africanism with a world-wide revolutionary movement. Total unity in their view, is the *sine qua non* of African progress. It is clearly stated that an effective advance towards modernization cannot be achieved without continent-wide political union. Nkrumah and Touré are leading exponents of continental political unity. The militant Pan-Africanists maintain authoritarian regimes with rigid socialist orientation in economic policy.

The dominant view among the moderates is that the development of individual African states is a necessary pre-condition to broader political union. They favor the development of political and economic systems which allow increased individual freedom. They seek to develop greater co-operation and collaboration with other African states while maintaining their former ties with the metropolitan powers. A majority of the moderate African states enjoy the *"expression française"* and are in some form of association with the EEC. The moderates assign firm priority to political stability as a pre-condition of both economic development and Pan-Africanism.

It is significant that there is some correlation between those African states bent on rapid modernization, and those oriented towards a militant Pan-Africanism. Nkrumah's and Touré's militant brand of Pan-Africanism, for example, can be seen as a weapon for modernization. Radical in their orientation, most vigorous in their demand for equality, conscious of the primacy of political solutions to the problem of development, ultra-Pan-Africanists have generally tended to be socialists and "positive neutralists."

Many of the African states' problems arising from internal political and economic conditions tend to be reflected in external policy. For example, when Nkrumah decided, as a matter of domestic policy, that Ghana's political stability could be achieved only as a larger part of Pan-Africanism, the doctrine of non-intervention became meaningless. The case of Ghana is not entirely unique; as in other instances, the pursuit of such ideological objectives involved the expenditure of considerable wealth on Pan-African political goals. At the overt level, Ghana provided refuge for African nationalists and dissatisfied African exiles, while still presenting the image of a prosperous and dynamic African state. The emphasis on internal unity—imposed at any cost—forces militant African leaders to focus on external affairs, while at the same time projecting on the African scene a monolithic African personality embracing a Pan-African posture. Ideology aside, this can be understood in terms of a compulsive drive to achieve rapid growth to close the gap with the developed states. Pan-Africanism serves as a distraction and an excuse to silence popular discontent arising from failure of governments to deliver the "promised" goods of development.

PAN-AFRICANISM: AN ASSESSMENT

There is general agreement among African leaders that some form of co-operation is necessary to insure the economic development and political stability of the African states. Like any movement which ascribes to political man an objective identity, however, Pan-Africanism has difficulties in accommodating itself to pragmatic necessities. Africans do not necessarily agree on generalities; and even when it exists, such agreement is not easily transformed into concerted action on specifics. Emotional vagaries, ideological diversities, and political emphases combine in the African acknowledgment that something must be done. But there is only limited agreement on the question of "what" and "how."

With the proliferation of independence among African states, the greatest threat to their existence and coexistence comes not from colonialism or neo-colonialism, but from themselves and from one another. They are threatened by subversion from within and without, by factionalism and succession, by continental quarrels and rivalries, and by the ever-present possibility of wars between neighbors. All are testing the fabric of their societies by zealous attempts at modernization. The need for continental integration of some form is obvious.

Having recognized the possibilities of regional co-operation, the African states found themselves working at cross-purposes. Both to meet immediate functional requirements and to pay token homage to the politically useful ideals of Pan-Africanism, they provided a framework of continental co-ordination which could at least order the chaos to a degree that some progress might be made.

The OAU operates across, as well as along, the functional, economic dimension of integration. The political sector of the OAU apparatus manages to serve the politics of both nationalism and Pan-Africanism. African states are very jealous of their newly won sovereignties, and the OAU is bound to the task of preserving them.

For federalists, the OAU offers a means of asserting their personal and ideological leadership in a continental movement. They are less concerned with their relatively secure domestic positions than with enhancing their trans-national prestige in the pursuit of unity.

The OAU also provides a way to harmonize the African states' concern with vital issues. It could also provide a united African front to assert and defend interests at home and abroad. It is evident that the OAU is primarily a bundle of potentials, loosely held together by African idealism.

The problem of realizing this potential involves the translation of ideals into political reality. And Pan-Africanism is intrinsically too vague, and its vocabulary too imprecise. The ideals of Pan-Africanism are assigned different meanings by the different African leaders.

The Pan-African concept of unity has taken on several different meanings. To the federalists, it means nothing less than an absolute federal union of the African states similar in form, at least, to the United States or Switzerland. Others interpret it as a unity of purpose which is expressed through voluntary co-operation in African affairs. Still others perceive it as a unity of aspirations to be practically expressed by a wide variety of methods. Also, there is virtually no agreement on the means to achieve unity. The various nationalistic regimes and movements have developed their own approaches to the same problem, and each is equally convinced that his method is the best and most appropriate.

Most African states are intoxicated with their independence and are extremely wary of any unproven association which might compromise their sovereignty. This attitude is demonstrated by a willingness to enter into regional arrangements with immediate neighbors having similar needs and values. The over-all federalistic approach has been gradually discarded in favor of loose functional co-operation. In such a way, the new states attempt to meet immediate necessities and still retain most of their freedom of action.

There are many African communities, but there is no African society. The physical and spatial aspects of continental Africa operate independently of any psychic and consensual basis. African history, confirmed in the recent African experience of secession and national rivalries, gives little evidence that Africa has the potential to respond as a unit. The various African states possess only the minimal attributes of national unity and share few common norms. It is doubtful that today's Africans can develop a dominant ideology or articulate a consistent, common response in the international system.

While African liberation movements crystallized desires for unity, the coming of independence magnified the will to retain national sovereignties. While the common drive for liberation made African unity a conceptual reality, the acquisition of independence transformed it into an operational myth. Pan-Africanism is a state of mind, not a state of affairs. Prior to independence the Africans had developed an over-romanticized concept of unity. When independence became a reality and unity was within easy reach, they found that they did not know what to do with it. This should not be surprising. In the process of evolution from the necessities of liberation to the wants of sovereignty, the Africans are experiencing a profound psychological change. This change is signified by the expansion of the African's area of choice, as well as by the exercise of his critical judgment. Also, the area of selection extends to means as well as to end-formulation. Hence, the difference between Nkrumah's and Senghor's path to Pan-Africanism becomes a living issue.

Africa has a very long way to go in translating Pan-Africanism from a mere logical possibility to a realistic probability. There can be no effective integration without common norms, and an African normative order becomes real only when the philosophy of the African leaders is not so far divorced from the values and assumptions held by the people that it loses all relevance. Under such conditions of diversity, Pan-Africanism can be little more than a politically useful myth.

NOTES

1. For an evaluation, see J. Crutcher, "Pan-Africanism: African Odyssey," *Current History*, January, 1963. Also, Rupert Emerson, "Pan-Africanism," *International Organization*, Spring, 1962.

2. For a commentary on the Brazzaville Conference, see Hella Pick, "The Brazzaville Twelve and How They Came to Be," *Africa Report*, XVI, No. 5, p. 2.

3. For a commentary on the Casablanca Conference, see *The Economist*, January 14, 1961, pp. 121-122.

4. Kwame Nkrumah, *Africa Must Unite* (London: Heinemann, 1963), p. 144.

5. For a commentary on the Monrovia Conference, see *The Economist,* May 20, 1961, p. 766.

6. See Appendix C: The Charter of the Organization of African Unity.

BIBLIOGRAPHY

American Society of African Culture. *Pan-Africanism Reconsidered.* Berkeley, Calif.: University of California Press, 1962.

BURKE, FREDERICK G. *Africa's Quest for Order.* Englewood Cliffs, N.J.: Prentice-Hall, 1964.

CARTER, GWENDOLEN M. (ed.). *National Unity and Regionalism in Eight African States.* Ithaca, N.Y.: Cornell University Press, 1966.

COX, RICHARD. *Pan-Africanism in Practice: PAFMECSA 1958-64.* London: Oxford University Press, 1964.

HUGHES, A. J. *East Africa: The Search for Unity.* Baltimore: Penguin Books, 1963.

LEGUM, COLIN. *Pan-Africanism.* New York: Frederick A. Praeger, 1962.

LEYS, COLIN AND PETER ROBSON (eds.). *Federation in East Africa: Opportunities and Problems.* New York: The Oxford University Press, 1966.

McKAY, VERNON (ed). *African Diplomacy: Studies in the Determinants of Foreign Policy.* New York: Frederick A. Praeger, 1966.

MEZRE, OKECHUKU (ed.). *The Philosophy of Pan-Africanism.* Washington, D.C.: The Georgetown University Press, 1965.

NKRUMAH, KWAME. *Africa Must Unite.* New York: Frederick A. Praeger, 1963.

———. *I Speak of Freedom.* New York: Frederick A. Praeger, 1961.

NYE, JOSEPH S. *Pan-Africanism and East African Integration.* Cambridge, Mass.: Harvard University Press, 1965.

PADMORE, GEORGE. *Pan-Africanism or Communism? The Coming Struggle for Africa.* New York: Roy Publishers, 1956.

QUAISON-SACKEY, ALEX. *Africa Unbound.* New York: Frederick A. Praeger, 1963.

SPIRO, HERBERT J. (ed.). *Patterns of African Development.* Englewood Cliffs, N.J.: Prentice-Hall, 1967.

TEVOEDJRE, ALBERT. *Pan-Africanism in Action: An Account of the U.A.M.* (Occasional Paper No. 2), Cambridge, Mass.: Harvard University Center for International Affairs, 1965.

WELCH, CLAUDE E., JR. *Dream of Unity: Pan-Africanism and Political Unification in West Africa.* Ithaca: N.Y.: Cornell University Press, 1966.

8 ·

Security through Neutralism *

Through the strategy of non-alignment Africa rejects the cold war international system. She transcends the split between East and West by adopting an ideology that is allegedly more relevant than the alternatives extended by either great power. The African ideology of non-alignment is permeated by the feelings of alienation and anomie experienced by "free" Africans. It reflects a variety of psycho-social sentiments including anxiety, futility, and moral and intellectual skepticism.

The principles and practices of African non-alignment have arisen in response to contemporary conditions of international politics as perceived by the African leaders. Their interpretation of the international political situation differs from both the Western and the Communist views.

Throughout its modern history, Africa has been the body upon which the rival great powers trampled. Today, however, antipathy between great powers has become vital to the existence of independent African states. In fact, the conditions of non-alignment have included two mutually exclusive and hostile

*The terms *neutralism* and *non-alignment* are used synonymously in this chapter. The traditional concept of *neutrality* is defined later in this discussion.

blocs headed by nuclear superpowers and the proliferation of small, weak, non-industrialized new states.

The final collapse of colonial empires in Africa during the 1950's and 1960's produced a power vacuum which both blocs sought to fill. Power tends to radiate outward from its central source and fill any area in which there is a power deficiency. But the same militant African nationalism that hastened the colonial demise could not but, for the most part, reject the overtures for bloc alignment.

The present posture of Africans in the international system is a function of their view of contemporary international politics. Many African attitudes toward international politics come from the search for a uniquely African identity and role in the world. These attitudes are also the natural result of African anti-colonialism. In following a course of non-alignment, African states are attempting to strengthen their individuality; in so doing, they are almost inevitably cast in a role between the major powers, but subservient to neither.

THE AFRICAN IMAGE
OF INTERNATIONAL POLITICS

Ever since their emergence as independent states, Africans have conceived their function to be one of setting the world straight. However much disagreement there might be over details, Africans have concurred that a unique responsibility for the peace and security of the entire world has devolved upon them.

From the beginnings of independence, a set of intellectual and operational assumptions has knit together the disparate strands of African foreign policies. These *a priori* foundations of Africa's decisions and actions have constituted the basis of her non-alignment ideology since the late fifties. They may be phrased as follows:

(1) Neo-colonialism poses the principal threat to African existence.

(2) The East-West conflict is merely a struggle for power and domination of smaller states.

(3) The bi-polar international system does not reflect African interests and objectives.

(4) Africa is uniquely suited to ameliorate the conditions of the international system.

Their own experiences have led African states to believe that colonialism as a world force is on the defensive, but they assert that it is merely the old forms of colonialism which are passing rapidly. In the concept of neo-colonialism as espoused by Nyerere, Nasser and others, Africans found further justification for jealously guarding their national independence. Foreign domination may take many new and insidious forms which are just as dangerous as the old.

Western critics are quick to point out what they think is an unwarranted African preoccupation with the outdated danger of Western domination. At the same time, many Westerners insist that the African states are blinded to the real threat of Communism by this preoccupation. Two facts are significant here. First, Western domination is a part of the immediate past of Africa and is connected to the highly emotional issue of racism and exploitation. Throughout the colonial period, Africa was a pawn of the West, controlled by the West with comparatively little regard for legitimate African interests and welfare. Second, the African leaders are, in fact, acutely conscious of the dangers of Soviet domination as is evidenced by their domestic suppression of Communist parties.

Africa quite naturally sought a position in the international system which would assure continued freedom from domination by any foreign power. Within the context of the cold war this has been a genuine policy alternative; the African states have had the opportunity of courtship by both camps while refusing marriage to either. This advantageous situation obviously depends on the continuation of great power rivalry and on the will of the African leaders. Their successes make it evident that their ability has been continuously underestimated by both East and West.

African states simply cannot see either Soviet Communism or democratic liberalism as a prime menace to their autonomy. It is, instead, the continuation of international political tensions which may eventually lead to their physical destruction or their subjection to a new foreign domination which concerns them most. And it is between this Scylla and Charybdis that they are trying to steer an independent course reflecting their own national interests.

African leaders recognize the possibility of major war as directly threatening their continued existence. The climate of international political tensions into which the new states were suddenly injected is not the most auspicious for their security. Both sides in the global struggle are potential sources of infringement on their sovereignty, and a nuclear war would destroy all their hopes for development.

It is a basic tenet of African leaders that they are able, by the very fact of their aloofness from any bloc, to contribute constructively to the lessening of international tensions. Their reasoning is that if Africa were to form ranks along bloc lines, a highly volatile situation would result. The world would be split into a tight bipolar pattern; there would be no group of mediators between the two antithetical poles, and freedom of movement—political fluidity—would virtually disappear. Under such conditions, conflict would be institutionalized, a *détente* would be much harder to achieve, and the possibilities for a disaster would multiply.

Successfully implemented policies of non-alignment, however, tend to retain and increase the fluidity of the system. Africans believe that the interplay of opinions, the expression of multiple interests, and the existence of mediating groups can have a definite effect on progress towards reduction of international tensions and prevention of nuclear war. In fact, many African leaders feel that because their continent is diversified in race, language and religion, ideology, and history, they can serve as an example of toleration and coexistence.

African leaders seem to have concluded that containment of the great powers is necessary for the maintenance of their sovereignty and for an over-all *détente*. To achieve this, they must work to prevent political, military, and economic dominance of Africa by either bloc; thus, they will create an "off-limits area" to the protagonists of the cold war. East and West must follow African dictates. This leads to a seesaw effect: Africans deal with both blocs, support one and then the other, all the while receiving massive aid from both and becoming subservient to neither. Cold war policies commonly followed in Europe and Asia cannot be implemented in Africa.

African leaders sometimes characterize their policies as expressions of an international conscience, or as elements of rationality which help to temper the predominance of irrationality on the international scene. Africans see themselves as having a special international mission to articulate the basic world desire for peace. They feel that through their positions of non-alignment, and because of their objectivity vis-à-vis the two blocs, they will be heard by all. They can assume this because they feel that they have no binding commitment to any one position, merely a vested interest in peaceful co-operation.

Starting from these basic attitudes, the African states have come to place great faith in international organizations. For example, they feel that the United Nations can and should exert a very strong influence in settling international disputes—even those among great powers. International organizations, like non-alignment itself, become vehicles for increasing the political power and influence of what traditionally would have been insignificant states. Africans, by various means, are literally attempting to force the great powers to pay them heed. They seek to develop a non-political international system in which distinctions between states are to be vitiated in favor of global co-operative efforts to relieve the material misery of the human race.

THE FUNCTIONS OF NON-ALIGNMENT

As translated from precept to practice, African non-alignment is designed to serve specific functions. Stripped to their essence, these include:

(1) Reconciliation between national sovereignty and the requirements of security;
(2) Harmonization between political independence and economic dependence;
(3) Maintenance and enhancement of national solidarity;
(4) Maximization of foreign policy alternatives and power in international politics;
(5) Establishment of an African role and identity in the international system.

African non-alignment must be distinguished from the traditional concept of neutrality, for there are striking differences. Neutrality is essentially a legal condition of a state's external relations which allows it to remain uninvolved in the international disputes or wars which are surging back and forth around it. It is passiveness, abstention, and even indifference to what is happening. A neutral state does not have official opinions on international matters; it does not even attempt to decide, for its own benefit, who is right and who is wrong. It takes no sides in any conflict, verbal or military, and maintains an officially equal attitude toward all belligerents. Neutral states are officially satisfied with whatever the status quo happens to be at the time. They have no demands to make on any other countries or blocs. This is not to say, however, that a neutral will not defend itself when attacked or when its vital interests are seen as being threatened.

Non-alignment, on the other hand, presupposes an international situation characterized by power blocs. A non-aligned state is one that has no binding military, political, or economic ties to a power center outside its borders. It formulates its foreign and domestic policies, insofar as it can, independently of any outside considerations of allies or bloc leaders. It has no obligations other than to its own definitions of its national interest, though it may carefully consider the effects of its actions on other states if it chooses to do so. It need never fear being pulled into a conflict where it might be forced to compromise its national interests, and it need never fear being regarded as an "enemy by association" by a state with which it has no quarrel.

From these distinctions it may be inferred that all neutral states, by definition, are non-aligned countries. The non-aligned states, however, have the choice of remaining truly neutral or of participating in technically non-neutral activities while maintaining a non-aligned status. It is precisely this element of choice, this freedom of decision, which the African states view as essential.

The non-aligned states of Africa carry on active foreign policies, both in direct contact with members of the two major blocs and through international organizations such as the United Nations. They have opinions and express them freely. To the extent that they are able to do so, they exert pressures for and against parties to disputes. They have even gone so far from the traditional concept of neutralism as to form *ad hoc* blocs of their own for the joint pursuit of common objectives. Yet, they remain absolutely unaligned with either major power center; their support, as stated above, may see-saw between the two as they take independent positions on issues and seek support from both sides or from other non-aligned states.

Among the non-aligned states of Africa, three main groups or types can be discerned. There are those who look primarily to the West for their forms of government, their ideological orientation, and aid for their development. Likewise, there are those states who look primarily to the Soviet Union for ideological identification and economic assistance. And, finally, there are those which appear to be trying consistently to remain aloof from both blocs while actively seeking aid from both. This last position is very difficult to maintain, but it may be the most effective in terms of both domestic benefits and international influence acquired.

Since the African states have attached an absolute quality to their independence, they take intense pride in both domestic and international self-reliance. They are loath to commit themselves to policies before they examine them in terms of their own national interests and goals. They fear that alignment with either bloc would commit them to future courses of action over which they would have little or no control; and that such future conditions could easily lead them into compromising their national interest.

Furthermore, non-alignment has a snowballing effect—it has become the fashionable position for new states. Great prestige has accrued to leaders among the non-aligned states, and the international influence of otherwise weak states can be strengthened effectively through non-aligned policies.

The leaders of the African states are quick to point out that non-alignment is not synonymous with ethical fence-sitting. As stated above, they view their position as the truest expression of an acute moral and idealistic sense, for they can and do judge the policies and actions of both blocs, then accept what they regard as beneficial or condemn what they find to be objectionable.

Africans have fully assumed the traditional international ideal of the sovereign state as a vehicle for expressing their own particular identities. Upon the achievement of political independence for their states, African nationalist leaders began to act as sovereign leaders have traditionally acted. The same militant nationalism which won independence was turned to an active defense and assertion of that independence. As the African states became determined to define their own national destinies without any outside pressures, anti-colonialist feelings were projected to include all types of foreign domination.

The immediate goal of the African states is national development, in short, modernization. They realize that this cannot be achieved alone; hence, the necessity of aid from industrialized states. But, they also recognize that economic dependence can lead to at least partial domination of their internal and external affairs by foreign powers. To avoid foreign control and maintain their sovereignty, while at the same time receiving massive amounts of aid from the great powers, has been the basic problem for the new African states. They have found a partial answer by seeking aid from all available sources, but in so doing have made it clear that their political allegiance is not for sale.

Inasmuch as both blocs view their aid programs as political weapons to stop the undue accretion of influence by the other, it has been possible for the African states to exploit both sides in the ideological struggle. By thus trading on the anxieties of East and West, African states have been able to obtain the required aid to further their development, yet remain aloof from alignment with either bloc.

The practical and immediate benefits of non-alignment are perhaps the most important and the most appreciated by African leaders. African states are in the enviable position of being able to virtually demand economic assistance from both sides in the cold war. Through a sort of blackmail, they can assure the continuation of aid from both sides, as long as each believes that its aid is serving the purpose of diminishing the influence of the other. This calls for some occasional fancy footwork, but some African leaders have proven that experience makes for a nearly perfect performance. Some have been receiving aid continuously from both the United States and the Soviet Union, and have been alternately lauding and damning both.

Non-alignment plays yet another important role for African states, a role that derives from domestic political considerations; it acts as a rallying point to mobilize widespread domestic support behind governmental actions vis-à-vis the external world. The nationalist elites who assumed political power when the colonial regimes departed are caught in the middle of domestic factional struggles. In the African states there are the elite groups which are closely identified with the values of the Western tradition due to their working contact with the former colonial regime and through Western education. Opposed to them are the ultra-nationalists, whose response to the outside world may border on xenophobic racism. The third group is usually quasi-Marxist, neo-Communist, or Socialist, and is generally inclined toward emulation of the Soviet or Chinese regimes.

To preserve an already tenuous and strained national unity, to create a national consciousness, and to progress along the road to promised development, the groups within the state require that the African leaders pursue policies which will satisfy each of them. This must be done to avoid the disaster of civil war or of domination through subservience to either bloc. Non-alignment seems to offer the African leaders just such a possibility. An assertive foreign policy, a demonstration of willingness to support, co-operate with, and receive aid from both blocs—all are attempts to satisfy the domestic power factions in the interest of unity. When Africans combine these factors with the common enemy of colonialism, they feel that they have arrived at a winning combination at home at the same time that they are serving their interests abroad.

Since the African states are trying to pursue foreign policies that are in response to their own national identities, needs, and desires, they realize that to maintain the greatest possible range of policy alternatives they have to be free to side with any state as the situational conditions vary. Their foreign policies are eminently consistent when seen not through the eyes of the United States or Soviet Union, but from the viewpoint of the national interest of the African states in question.

In terms of political strategy, non-alignment is one of two choices that are open to African states—choices which are both the result of weakness vis-à-vis the great powers. Some states, realizing their very vulnerable positions, have opted for alignment with a bloc. But this is not to imply that the non-aligned African states do not realize their vulnerability, as some Western critics would have us believe.

On the contrary, the African states, fully aware of their position vis-à-vis both blocs, have decided that non-alignment offers them the best possibility of maintaining and developing their national identities in the face of the global hostilities which surround them. Instead of choosing between the real powers, they have decided to try to improvise an alternative which will maximize their operational choices, and give them the greatest opportunities for independent pursuit of their own national interests.

For Africa, non-alignment is a means of gaining strength through weakness. African states can exploit their economic and political positions. Their diplomatic voices continuously work to lessen the importance of military power in international politics, and as the importance of force declines, their influence rises.

The non-aligned states of Africa are constantly trying to justify their neutralist position to the rest of the world. Pressures from Moscow, Peking, and Washington are denounced. Charges of "expediency" are heatedly denied. Africa repeats over and over again that it is primarily concerned with its own interests, collective and individual, and that non-alignment is the only course open.

African leaders have thus concluded that it is in their national interest to act as a mediating force between the two antagonists. Their goal is the creation of an international political system which avows coexistence as a basic value, tolerates diverse ideologies, and allows and fosters free development of their own African states along the lines they desire.

Undoubtedly, idealistic concerns for world peace, for mediating the cold war, and for eliminating the use of force in international politics play a part in determining the outlines of African non-alignment. There is a feeling in Africa that the existence of a definite group of non-aligned states who have no vested interest in the power of either major bloc is the only hope for a truly objective solution to the problems caused by international tensions. African states feel that both blocs will recognize their impartiality in disputes and will accept mediation efforts from Africa or from the United Nations. From time to time, this feeling has led to calls for the formation of a neutralist bloc, in the hope that such a concert would be able to bring effective pressure on parties in conflict, and result in a mediated settlement.

THE MYTH OF THE "AFRO-ASIAN BLOC"

Since the rise of territorial states out of the political vacuum that was medieval Europe, men have tried to go beyond the balance of power by enforcing systematic norms. Emerging victorious from the Second World War, Russia and the United

States attempted to consolidate the states of the world into two rigid systems. The cold war period was both pleasing and frustrating to the great powers. Direct interaction between them was limited to ideological rites, with neither side gaining more than an occasional dubious victory.

Even before they emerged from under the aegis of colonialism, the new Afro-Asian states were politically, economically, militarily, and ideologically accosted by Moscow and Washington. Rather than succumbing to the bi-polarized configuration of power, however, Asians and Africans opted for a non-aligned political course.

Non-alignment was conceived by Nehru as a tactic arising from India's strategic needs. The concept soon acquired a hallowed glow in the capitals of new states around the globe. Furthermore, it became a rallying point for Afro-Asian solidarity. While non-Western leaders shunned commitment to the existing blocs, many sought to bring the non-West into world politics as a "third force."

In 1955 the independent Afro-Asian states met at Bandung under the tutelage of Nehru. They expressed a concerted opinion regarding the evils of colonialism and the desirability of nationalism and socialism. They extended friendship to their sister state, China. It appeared that the "spirit of Bandung" would transform the non-West into a world-wide political actor.

A series of Afro-Asian solidarity conferences of governments, peoples, parties, labor unions, and students followed during the next decade. Nasser in 1957, Nkrumah in 1958, Touré in 1960, and Tito in 1961 were among their vociferous sponsors. However, the rhetoric of these meetings—the denunciations of colonialism and neo-colonialism, and the expressed desires to mediate the cold war—became increasingly divorced from the realities of world politics.

Whereas in 1958 Ghana and Ethiopia were the lone sub-Saharan African states in the non-aligned bloc, by the end of 1965 there were thirty-four. Not only did the complete emergence of Africa from colonial status destroy the basis of the anti-colonialist barrages; it also destroyed the myth of Afro-Asian solidarity projected from Bandung. As the Afro-Asian states achieved independence, they found they had diverse opinions and interests. China's invasion of India in 1963 demolished the pretense that Afro-Asians even adhered to the principle of coexistence; China's denunciation of the Nuclear Test Ban Treaty of 1963 dispelled further the image of the compromising and placid non-Western soul.

Furthermore, neutralism as the basis of Afro-Asian solidarity was relevant only as long as the bipolarization of international power was a fact. Polycentrism is evident today in the Eastern and Western camps; China and Rumania, France and Pakistan, are the vociferous malcontents in the Russian and American blocs. This situation leaves the mediator without a function. African foreign ministers become lonelier as the great and lesser powers pursue their national interests without respect for bloc or ideological commitments.

The embarrassingly abrupt end of the Afro-Asian conference at Algiers in 1965 was symptomatic of the demise of the "third force." Yet, it merely dramatized what most African and Asians had long suspected: that Afro-Asian solidarity, if ever a reality, had become a myth like that of the "free world" or the "Communist bloc." Unlike these latter phenomena, however, there was no great power to constrain fragmentation. At Algiers it was openly acknowledged that the alleged solidarity had not been subverted by neo-colonial forces, but rather divided by the stresses of changing conditions and conflicting national interests. In Afro-Asia, as in the West, in the absence of substantive systemic norms, the realities of sovereign states burst the myth of unity.

NON-ALIGNMENT: AN ASSESSMENT

Non-alignment is the logical result of African acceptance of the traditional doctrine of sovereignty, and of attempts to apply it to contemporary international conditions. It arises from the doctrine of sovereign independence and from the African's passionate attachment to an absolute aura or mystique of state freedom.

The prime characteristic of the contemporary international system is that no state, not even one of the great powers, can act solely on the basis of its own narrowly-interpreted interests. The few exceptions of naked unilateral intervention by states in the post-1945 period, such as the Russian crushing of the Hungarian revolt, or the American war in Vietnam, prove this rule. Absolute independence is now utterly out of the question. State action must result from a careful analysis of the effects it will produce on the other states and on the international system as a whole. Very real limits are placed on the scope and nature of state ends and means.

Yet, precisely at the time when sovereignty and independence of action are becoming anachronistic, and when an assertion of such an absolute conception of sovereignty borders on irresponsibility, the African states have become intoxicated with the idea. Since achieving independence, the first objective of the African states has been to preserve and assert independence. It is jealously guarded and vociferously argued; any attempts, real or imagined, by a foreign government to encroach on its absoluteness are met with near-violent reactions and bitter denunciations.

African neutralism and claims of uniqueness serve a vital internal function and project themselves outwards into the international system largely as a posture of convenience and profit. Claims of uniqueness can possibly be traced back to a deep sense of insecurity; in fact this very stressing of their uniqueness may serve only to slow down the process of modernization in the African states. Rejection of all things Western in favor of a real or imagined uniquely African heritage, culture, and value system can only prove detrimental to present and future attempts at development. African concern must be less with the trappings of sovereignty and more with the practical and real problems associated with modernization.

What African states apparently do not realize, or perhaps do not wish to admit to themselves, is that global interdependence is a fact. Any adjustment or action in one place will have consequences in another. Any action by a great power will affect, in some way, every other state. These conditions are bound to impose limitations on the sovereignty of all states; however, the African states cannot accept this fact.

One of the maxims of international conduct is: "Do what you can, and be prepared to suffer the consequences if you must." The African states, however, are trying to do much more than they actually can, and refuse to suffer any consequences at all.

The existence of competing blocs has helped make possible the African juggling act. So far, Africa has been able to exploit the anxieties of both East and West in such a way as to maximize the economic and political benefits to herself and to minimize her loss of freedom.

In one sense, African non-alignment is an elaborate rationale for a policy of exploitation. By "playing hard to get," Africa is assured of short-term benefits. The calculations of the African states seem to be based on the hope that by the time conditions have changed enough to negate the possibilities of such exploitation, they either will not need further aid for development, or else the aid will be naturally forthcoming through institutionalized international co-operation.

Such an assumption is the direct result of two basic premises: (1) either cold war competition will continue in its classical post-1945 form, enabling the exploitation of the split to continue; or (2) the major cold war issues will be settled, leading to a period of free international co-operation for development.

Africans see their course of non-alignment as meeting whatever contingencies might result from either of the two above conditions. Non-alignment is a sort of insurance policy against the future which pays immediate dividends as well. By not committing themselves to either side, they can use both for their own purposes as long as possible. If, through some unforeseen course of events, one side gains a dominant position in the struggle, Africa will not be tainted by association with the loser.

African diplomatic maneuvers in the United Nations and through other international organizations serve a similar purpose. They are designed to defend the argument that co-operative development and advancement are duties of the modern states. The wealthy states ought to help the poor ones to gain a similar position. Such efforts to institutionalize aid programs—national and international—are obvious.

However much the African states may be idealistically concerned with the peace of the world and with co-operation, their prime consideration is obviously their own progress and development. Having decided that their goal is the creation of a modern, industrialized nation-state, the Africans logically have asked themselves: What is the best way to get us from where we are to where we want to go? The years of bitter anti-colonialist nationalism, plus their absolute ideas about sovereignty, precluded alignment with either bloc. Following the lead of India, Burma, and others, they chose non-alignment.

In spite of all its virtues for the African states, ambitious non-alignment is potentially dangerous, for these states are essentially disjointed, faction-ridden, weak, and underdeveloped. By assuming unjustified and disproportionate political influence in relation to their actual capacities and strengths, Africans could easily be lured into a position of trying to use power and influence which they do not in fact have. Such an inflated sense of importance and power is very satisfying to peoples who are used to being treated as inferiors, and it is very useful in domestic politics. But, it could also be explosive.

BIBLIOGRAPHY

BRECHER, MICHAEL. *The New States of Asia: A Political Analysis.* New York: Oxford University Press, 1963.

CRABB, CECIL V. *The Elephants and the Grass: A Study of Non-Alignment.* New York: Frederick A. Praeger, 1965.

DIA, MAMADOU. *The African Nations and World Solidarity.* Translated by Mercer Cook. New York: Frederick A. Praeger, 1961.

JANSEN, G. H. *Nonalignment and the Afro-Asian States.* New York: Frederick A. Praeger, 1966.

KAHIN, GEORGE M. *The Asian-African Conference.* Ithaca, N.Y.: Cornell University Press, 1956.

LEGUM, COLIN. *Bandung, Cairo, and Accra.* Washington, D.C.: Public Affairs Press, 1957.

MARTIN, LAWRENCE (ed.). *Neutralism and Nonalignment.* New York: Frederick A. Praeger, 1962.

McKAY, VERNON. *Africa in World Politics.* New York: Harper and Row, 1963.

NKRUMAH, KWAME. *Neo-colonialism: The Last Stage of Imperialism.* New York: International Publishers, 1965.

POWER, PAUL F. (ed.). *Neutralism and Disengagement.* New York: Charles Scribner's Sons, 1964.

SCHATTEN, FRITZ. *Communism in Africa.* New York: Frederick A. Praeger, 1966.

THIAM, DOUDOU. *The Foreign Policy of African States.* New York: Frederick A. Praeger, 1965.

9 ·

Africa's Impact upon the International System

The emergence of the non-Western African states has had an undeniable, yet not easily measurable, impact on international politics. In the past, the international system has undergone considerable change and readjustment. In this sense, the emergence of numerous new states poses simply *another* challenge to a system fully accustomed to challenge and sufficiently flexible to respond.

It is readily apparent, however, that two crucial differences make the African states' impact on the system unique. Most evident is the more than doubled number of actors on the international scene since 1945. The international political stage has been beset by a virtual horde of new "bit players" whose demands for prominent roles remain unfulfilled. At the same time, the number of "lead players" has been drastically reduced. Prior to 1945 the system seldom, if ever, faced the task of so quickly absorbing changes of such far-reaching consequence.

The second crucial difference between past and present challenges to the system is the nature of the challengers, as perceived by the system itself. The numerous and culturally dissimilar Afro-Asian states are too handily identified by the established members of the system as obviously "non-Western." But, to lump the new states together into such a facile category clearly demonstrates the magnitude and meaning of the Western world's misunderstanding of, and maladjustment to, the new challengers.

When confronted by the unfamiliar, an individual tends to react in a manner which least disturbs his sense of self. He is especially inclined to apply his own self-image as a criterion of comparison in the evaluation of others and is often satisfied with the conclusion that "they" are somehow "different." The peoples of the Western world have reacted with such pattern of behavior to the unfamiliar aspects of the new African states. Because the Western peoples are not yet capable of isolating and identifying the positive aspects of the African states, the underdeveloped states are negatively perceived as non-Western in their heritage, their value and belief systems, and their orientation to their own societies and to the rest of the world. As no longer tractable dependencies or colonies, the new states clearly fail to fit the collective Western self-image and are automatically assigned to the antithetical category—the "non-West."

THE IDEOLOGIES OF AFRICAN UNIQUENESS

As a creation of the Western world, the international system reflects the values, beliefs, ideals, realities, and experiences of those nations normally referred to as "Western." (It should be noted here that "Western" is employed not as a geographical designation, but as a label under which all nations sharing basic characteristics are included. The Soviet Union, for example, comes under this category.) The peoples and states of non-Western origin and heritage have only recently come to play—or attempt to play—a significant and independent role in world affairs. For centuries, the "relations of states" was taken to mean—and in a very real sense could only be conceived as meaning—the relations between Western states. Political relations between the West and other parts of the world were usually the result of pressures by a particular Western state against one or more non-Western peoples. There was, therefore, no established pattern of interaction between the West and the non-West.

In the years prior to general independence in Africa, nationalism provided the most effective driving force for political action, and anti-colonialism served as the keystone of nationalism. It provided by far the most solid and most central basis for nationalistic fervor. It was necessary for African leaders to provide their cadres and their peoples with an ideal around which they could rally and in the service of which they could establish unity. Though independence was stressed as a positive goal, it derived much of its appeal from the negative vector of anti-colonialism. Indeed, history, suggests that it is far simpler—and far more effective—to unify the masses and arouse them to action by emphasizing the necessity of eradicating an evil, than by stressing the desirability of establishing a new order. Elimination of an existing visible enemy, destruction of the "old order," provides a people with an immediate and readily perceived objective. The often vague and nebulous concept of national identity is less easily grasped, requires projection into the future, and cannot, by itself, adequately sustain mass action. In the pre-independence period, then, anti-colonialism was employed as a tool with which to forge and enforce nationalism.

In the post-independence period, anti-colonialism lost its effectiveness as an adequate support of the artificial and essentially negative nationalism of the new African states. But the old slogans of anti-colonialism were not completely discarded. They were employed instead in the performance of a new function and in the service of a new cause. Convinced that anti-colonialism was a useful weapon in their own struggles toward independence, the new African states continued to generate anti-colonialist propaganda for consumption by the peoples of the remaining colonial areas of Africa. In doing so, African leaders sought to project an image of themselves as champions of *all* dependent Africans, as outspoken supporters of *all* independence movements, and as fearless enemies of colonialism everywhere. Thus, in the post-independence period, the anti-colonialist ideology diminished in importance as a domestic issue. However, the externalization of anti-colonialism created an internal ideological void which had to be filled. It was vitally necessary to produce new ideological foundations if an adequate level of nationalistic fervor was to be maintained. Though the anti-colonialist brand of nationalism and the imminence of independence succeeded in the temporary political unification of diverse and frequently antagonistic internal forces and groups, the actual achievement of independence removed the driving force behind national unification.

Therefore, the ghost of colonialism has been revived to provide a focal point for the forces of African nationalism. With its form and content revised to meet present needs and to conform to present circumstances, anti-colonialism has been refashioned as neo-colonialism. The new ideology provides today's leaders of the independent African states with an effective device with which to sustain old feelings and to generate new enthusiasms for national unity among their peoples. With a full appreciation of the historical effectiveness of a real or imagined external threat to sovereignty and independence as a means of maintaining internal unity and cohesion, the new ideology consists more in the ascription of residual colonial ambition than in active opposition to actual colonial pressures. The essentially ascriptive nature of the new focus of African nationalism is implicit in the semantic construction of the term most commonly used to describe it—*neo*-colonialism, rather than *anti*-colonialism.

This is not to suggest that every leader of a newly independent African state has cynically exploited anti-colonialist and neo-colonialist slogans. Undoubtedly, some leaders respond sincerely to what they feel are real and tangible threats to their states' existence as free and independent entities. Sincerity, however, is not the most convincing characteristic of leadership groups; the more ambitious leaders of the African states are well practiced in the manipulation of neo-colonialist slogans for the attainment of other goals and objectives. And so it is necessary to determine whether there is any real neo-colonialist threat to African sovereignty, or whether such fears and charges stem from a basic lack of realism in the African leaders' perception of the world about them. The latter explanation seems to correspond more accurately to the facts of international life.

As has been suggested above, one of the more important operational factors in the contemporary international system is the increasing interdependence of states and peoples. No state today is totally independent. The degree of political, social, economic, and cultural independence varies from state to state, but none is completely sovereign. The new states of Africa have tended to ignore this reality of international life. Having only recently won their political independence, they jealously and fearfully guard their new status. In their concern to maintain that status, they fail to perceive the relativity of independence. They tend to interpret the necessities of interdependence as dangerous threats to their national identities. In many cases, they are driven by the compulsion to display their social, economic, and cultural *uniqueness* to the rest of the world.

The new states claim to be fearful of penetration and takeover by their former colonial masters. Furthermore, any form or degree of penetration of their societies by a member of the Western world is interpreted as an encroachment upon their sovereignties. Charges of neo-colonialism are directed against the United States, as well as against the traditional European colonialists. The United States has been judged by many Africans to be guilty of neo-colonialism by virtue of its ties and associations with Europe and its short-lived imperialist adventures in other parts of the world at the close of the nineteenth century. And because the United States is clearly stronger and more powerful than any of its European allies, it usually is assigned a position high on the list of those powers which are to be watched and dealt with cautiously.

As a result of these attitudes, the new African states draw a clear-cut distinction between "modernization" and "Westernization;" they deny any degree of congruence between the two concepts. All the new states seek to modernize themselves, to build viable economies, to establish new political institutions— to become, in a word, a part of the developed world. This intense concern with rapid development is clearly evidenced throughout Africa. Enormous and expensive dams, shiny new steel mills, and unnecessarily extensive airlines and shipping lines are only the more conspicuous manifestations of this preoccupation with modernization. Relatively little effort is directed to the less ostentatious, but more essential, requirements of modern state development. The reason for this obsession with the conspicuous is obvious. The vast physical and fiscal dimensions of dam construction projects add immeasurably to their usefulness as symbols of modernization. In contrast, long-range conservation programs are not as exciting to the imagination, nor do they lend themselves to direct, visual appreciation by the masses of the people. And it is not only for the benefit of the peoples of their own countries that the more flamboyant showpiece projects are selected: the developing African states are equally concerned with impressing the West.

In addition to its function as a prestige symbol, modernization is recognized by contemporary African leadership as a useful means of strengthening the forces of internal cohesion. It can serve to maintain popular passions, loyalties, and willingness to make sacrifices. And these, of course, are essential ingredients of a fully developed sense of national consciousness.

Westernization, on the other hand, has been singled out for attack. It is interpreted by Africa as a value-laden concept, whereas modernization is perceived as a neutral term, devoid of all such connotations. Modernization is seen as the heart of the African problem, while Westernization is dismissed as inappropriate to the African environment. Africa is, in effect, saying to the West: "We seek to be as modern as you are, but we reject your mode of development in favor of a form or forms which we ourselves will determine and which will reflect our own heritage and cultural patterns." In this fashion, anti-Westernization is promoted for both internal and external consumption. And as a corollary of modernization, it contributes effectively to the intensity of nationalism in the new African states.

The remaining facet of contemporary African nationalism is neutralism. The projection of a neutralist image is equally important as a means of enhancing the prestige of African leadership and of increasing the sense of national identity. Commitment to either bloc of the contemporary bi-polar configuration of the international system is interpreted as weakness; however, non-alignment is conceived as an expression of both the will and the ability to stand alone as a people and as a state. The prestige factor is a crucial one, and the fact that non-alignment encourages, rather than discourages, the cheerful acceptance of material assistance from any and all sources does not diminish its effectiveness as a manipulative political tool. The state posture of non-alignment continues to reflect the forces of nationalism which were implicit in the slogans and policies of anti-colonialism and neo-colonialism, and it retains the driving force of modernization without commitment to Westernization.

THE AFRICAN SYSTEM

In its simplest terms, nationalism can be defined as a sense of unity. But the development of such a sense of "we-ness" depends heavily upon a contrasting development of the notion of "they." The weaker the "we-group" orientation, the greater the need for a distinctively identifiable, and often arbitrary, notion of "they." For a people to recognize and acknowledge shared values, and a common heritage, goals, and objectives, they must be made to believe that these shared elements somehow distinguish them from other peoples who possess *different* goals, objectives, aspirations, and value and belief patterns. In many of the new African states, the sense of "we-ness" is extremely weak. The peoples of Nigeria, for example, are characterized as much by diversity as by unity. No single value or belief system is acceptable to all Nigerians; there is little or no common identity, nor shared goals and objectives, among the three principal tribes, Hausas, Ibos, and Yorubas. Rapid, enforced modernization of some sectors of the economy, the existence of antagonistic tribal groupings, and the emergence of an elite radically different from the masses of the people: all serve as actual or potential disruptive and disintegrative elements. In such a country, the "they" concept is emphasized in the hope that a positive sense of "we" will ultimately emerge.

Other African states, with similar deficiencies in the real and positive underpinnings of nationalism, have adopted different courses of action. They seek to stress the mythical or mystical, rather than the real, foundations of nationalism. They constantly refer to elusive and nebulous concepts of their "uniqueness," "cultural awakening," *negritude,* or "African Personality," but are careful to avoid any meaningful clarification or definition of these terms as a means of acquiring a reasonable degree of national consciousness. The value of these concepts lies chiefly in their abstract appeal to sentiments and loyalties which transcend internal antagonisms.

But, at the same time that a majority of African leaders are attempting to consolidate the diversities within their states and enthusiastically to assert their sovereignties, the Western powers are taking steps to divest themselves of many traditional prerogatives. African attempts to alter significantly the structure of the continent's international system have thus far failed. Functional integration is occurring in the West, not in Africa. The political landscape of the new Africa is littered with the debris of abandoned integration schemes. The West African case is typical. Immediately after Ghana achieved its independence in 1957, Nkrumah established a Bureau of African Affairs to promote the organization of a West African Federation in order to prevent the expected balkanization of West Africa. The passing of a full decade finds Nkrumah a political exile and West African federation no closer to political reality. Old conflicts and new tensions among the West African states have precluded any real progress towards political integration.

A major impediment to any level of African integration is irredentism. Because tribes are situated often in east-west layers across the generally north-south alignment of African states, they are frequently dismembered by political boundaries. This pattern of perpendicular ethno-political axes frequently results in mutual recrimination between states concerning the issue of tribal nationalities.

Nkrumah charges that the Ivory Coast's inhabitants are not appreciated by that country's leader, Houphouet-Boigny. Nkrumah has been suspected of harboring expansionist ideas when he has asserted that Ghana would ". . . pursue vigorously the reunification of the Nzimas and the Sanwis in the Ivory Coast with their brothers and sisters in Ghana."[1] Nkrumah's former neighbor to the east, Olympio of Togo, was alienated by Nkrumah's comment that: "Togo and Ghana are one and no amount of lies and deception to the people of Togoland can disprove this fact."[2] Tension also exists between Cameroon and Nigeria over the status of the inhabitants of the northern portion of the former British Cameroons.

Political tensions also plague East and Central Africa. The Federation of the Rhodesias and Nyasaland, formed in 1953, collapsed when each of its components achieved individual statehood in 1964. This was forecast by a leading American political scientist as early as 1962:

> One important federation which seems sure to break up is the Federation of Rhodesia and Nyasaland which has been bitterly fought by the African community particularly in Northern Rhodesia and Nyasaland since its origin in 1953. As African

majorities take over in these countries the hostility to the links which bind them to Southern Rhodesia will presumably make the maintenance of the existing federal structure impossible, although a new scheme of African inspired organization may emerge, perhaps within the broader framework offered by PAFMECSA.[3]

The failure of this integration scheme was almost guaranteed by the latent hostility between the dominant or soon-to-be dominant Negro elements in Northern Rhodesia and Nyasaland. Another integration effort, Julius Nyerere's Pan-African Freedom Movement in East, Central, and Southern Africa, has been unable to cope with the ethno-political complexities of the high lakes region of East Africa. To the northeast, Somalia is embroiled in a dispute with its neighboring states over the status of Somalia-inhabited borderlands namely, the Ogaden region of southeastern Ethiopia and Kenya's northeast.

Political integration in the Arab areas of Africa has been equally unsuccessful. One of the earliest North African attempts began with the signing of the Maghrebian Charter by the leadership of three Tunisian and Moroccan political parties in 1945. Algerian representatives joined Morocco and Tunisia in affirming the political interdependence of the three states at the Tangiers Conference of 1958. Tunisia's constitution imposes the duty of working for a Greater Maghrebian political entity; Morocco and Algeria assert that their territorial dispute should not be allowed to endanger Maghrebian consolidation. But beyond these expressions of intent, the newly-independent states of northwest Africa have taken no concrete steps towards integration.

Indeed, the entire Maghreb is wracked with interstate bickering. Morocco and Tunisia are at cross-purposes over Mauritania: while Tunisia recognized Mauritania's independence, Morocco seeks to "recover" it. Tunisia's Bourguiba has charged that Hassan of Morocco is interfering in Tunisia's domestic affairs by subversively encouraging Bourguiba's political opponents. Algerian and Moroccan troops have clashed in a border dispute over the Tindouf regions of extreme western Algeria; and the Moroccan government has accused the latest Algerian leader, Houari Boumedienne, of exporting Algerian revolutionary socialism in an attempt to destroy the Moroccan People's Monarchy. In a final permutation of Maghrebian political conflict, Tunisia and Algeria continue to quarrel over the

Saharan corridor claimed by the former in the region of Edgele, between Bir Romani and Marker 233 in Algeria's territory.

The Sudan is another African state burdened with the dual aspects of the problem of national identity. The Sudanese government has energetically asserted its sovereignty in two serious disputes with Egypt: an extended quarrel over control of the upper Nile and the short-lived Egyptian occupation, in 1958, of two areas along the northern Sudanese territory in connection with Egypt's military adventure in Yemen. But the problem of Sudanese internal diversity is so extreme that it completely overshadows her difficulties with Egypt or any other state. Central Sudan is the arena of the deepest encounter between the Arab world and the world of Black Africa; the Sudanese contrast between the northern, Arabic-speaking, Nubian Muslims and the generally animistic, negroid Nilotes forms a sharper cultural cleavage than is found anywhere else in Africa. And the task of containing, much less harmonizing, such internal diversity is formidable. Though the response of Sudanese nationalism to constant Egyptian pressures is insufficient to overcome the disruptive forces of internal diversity, Sudan is hardly inclined toward political integration with her dominant northern neighbor.

The emergence of the new African states has not forced a change in the traditional international system. The new Africa is, in fact, perpetuating the traditional state system structure at the very time that the traditional system is breaking down.

It is fruitful to inquire whether the kind of tensions and conflicts arising between the non-West and West today are substantially different from those which arose between the states of the traditional international system prior to the emergence of the non-West. Just as the control of raw materials in the Saar was a source of Franco-German conflict in the decades which preceded the European Coal and Steel Community of 1952, so the Moroccans and Algerians have conflicting claims with regard to the oil-rich regions of the Sahara. The irredentist causes of nineteenth century Italian statesmen caused conflict within the Austro-Hungarian empire; today, Ghana seeks to recover its Ewe "brethren" in Togo. Religious separatism figured significantly in the various Irish rebellions and has its contemporary parallel in the Muslim-Christian-pagan conflict in the Sudan. Control of strategically significant areas was the objective of both the British and Spanish as they fought over Gibraltar in 1713 and 1799; the same basic issue underlined the Suez crisis in 1956. Control of trading rights was an objective of France and Britain as they carried their European conflicts into colonial areas in the 1700's; the same objective embroils the Arabs and Israel in Africa today. The containment versus the promotion of subversion underlined tension between Republican France and other continental states during the Belgian succession in 1830; the same conflicting objectives have caused tension among the African states over political subversion by Communist China in Africa. Thus, it appears that the nature of conflict occasioned by the emergence of the non-West is not different in kind from that which typified international conflict in its previous European setting.

The structure remains familiar; the conflict seems ordinary. What of the historical significance of the states themselves? In broad historical perspective, it seems that the emerging African states' reaction to the intrusion of new values follows the historical pattern set by the traditional societies of Europe. By its very nature, nationalism is a vehicle of finite rather than universal values. And the new states serve the same particularistic, value-maximizing function that was the *raison d'être* of all European nationalist movements and the states they created.

The nationalist movements of nineteenth century Europe had the immediate goal of displacing alien monarchies with republican, locally oriented governments. But the emergent bourgeoisie simultaneously pursued an internally pluralistic goal: the breakdown of aristocratic control over the economy and polity so that the rationalization of these dimensions of life could proceed according to middle-class standards.

In the recent African experience, the democratization of society by means of increased commercial participation and secular education was accompanied by the emergence of a new elite that desired to displace the traditional order. Thus, the political emergence of the new African states operates well within the generic framework of most modern revolutions. In the sense that the African political elites are attempting to "nativize" their economies, industrialize, educate the masses, and suppress tribalism, they are responding to the same revolution in thought that has accelerated the development of modern civilization. Because of arbitrary boundaries, ethnic diversities, and fresh memories of colonialism—in short, the African situation—their efforts at modernization are excessively diverse in approach. However, the essential point is that the African state serves as a vehicle for a new and freshly value-oriented political elite.

In contrast, the Western states have become administratively dominant: they assist or protect *continuing* value satisfaction. With the decline of the old, particularistic values as a result of an increase in education, communication, cultural exchange, and widespread cosmopolitanism, the Western states have shed much of their original value-maximizing function. The values they now assert are materialistic; and materialistic values are more readily harmonized. The particularistic, value-maximizing attitude of the African states gives them a different sense of purpose from that of the modern Western state. It is this attitude, now becoming a thing of the recent past in the Western world, that perpetuates the meaning of nationhood today. In short, the new African states have given the concept of the nation-state a new lease on life.

Therefore, the phenomenon of the emerging non-West can be largely understood in the light of the historical development of world politics. Unified theories of international politics or partial generalizations have not been affected by the emergence of Africa, while analysis and comparisons of national development have gained new prominence in the literature of international political science. There are many novel features of the new states which have had little, if any, bearing on theory, but great import for policy sciences. This is not to say that these novelties will never affect theory construction—they may—it is merely to say that the African ecology makes it difficult to predict African state behavior. This, in turn, creates a problem for analysis.

The newly independent African states obviously lack the traditional broadly based nationalist underpinnings of the older European and American states. They are changing more rapidly and do not possess the working institutions of the Western states. Therefore, many of the traditional constants upon which past predictions of state behavior were based, especially predictions concerning state "objectives" rather than "goals," are missing. It is true, of course, that a similar, but less formidable, difficulty applies to the objectives of Western states—but for different reasons. In any case, both the foreign policy planner and the scholar, particularly those with an interest in Africa, find it upsetting to be without the traditional tools of their predictive trades. They are compelled to search for new constants in an effort to increase their predictive capabilities; hence, the current emphasis on analysis rather than theory building, a trend which is manifested in the recent development of "functionalism" in comparative politics.

A VIEW OF THE FUTURE

The African world has not settled upon a clearly organized attitude toward the West. Whether it is rational neutrality, in the case of the uncommitted, or simply confused state leadership, the point is that Africa finds it difficult to identify, much less articulate, her proper role in the world.

The international system was characterized above as a distinctly *Western* system, and as a system currently adjusting to internally precipitated or directed changes. Two crucial developments were emphasized: the far-reaching drive towards integration, and the growing interdependence of states. These are, of course, closely related phenomena, and they suggest that the system will continue to undergo fundamental changes in the next two or three decades. For example, it can be expected that new and varying types of regional organizations will emerge, and that the military function of existing international organizations will be displaced by developmental functions.

It can be safely assumed that the operational system of the foreseeable future—though fundamentally different in some respects from that which exists today—will remain a distinctly *Western* system. The major forces of change and readjustment are centrifugal and derive most of their energy from the Western world. And it can be expected that the evolving system will continue to reflect its original *Western* orientation.

What then of the impact of the African and other non-Western nations who are only now seeking to establish their place and assume their roles within the international political system? Two effects of their impact have already been discussed: the greatly increased number of actors on the international scene, and the emergence to a place of prominence of peoples with a distinctly non-Western background. It was argued further that the non-Western states bring to the international political scene two forces which currently operate in direct opposition to interdependence and integration: rigidly defined independence and contrived ideologies of uniqueness.

It is clear that the new states will, in the short run, exert some pressure for change on the system. They will continue, for example, to raise new issues and question the relevance of others. It is probable, however, that the impact of the non-West in the system will be both limited in time and peripheral in effect. Africa is not capable of drastically altering the system or forcing it to change the direction of its development. The forces of integration and interdependence are strong enough, and their momentum high enough, to oppose and eventually overcome the non-Western forces of uniqueness and independence. In the long-run, the *Western* system—whatever its future form—will force Africa to change, to adjust, and to conform.

Despite their loudly voiced claims to the contrary, the African states will find it impossible to modernize without becoming more and more Westernized. The very direction and intensity of their preoccupation with modernization acts to accelerate the Westernizing process; each developmental goal achieved is an intermediate step towards Westernization.

As they continue to operate within the international system and involve themselves in increased contacts and more complex relationships with the western states, the African states will necessarily respond to forces within the system; in doing so, they will begin to conform to the Western pattern. They will find it virtually impossible to maintain their imagined separateness from a system of increasingly integrated, supranational actors. As modernizing members of the system, they will eventually discover that independence is a relative term and that the characteristic interdependence of the system is inescapable—and profitable as well.

The Western system was superimposed upon Africa for a full colonial century, roughly 1850 to 1950. During this period, Africa was dominated by the Western states and played no independent international role. Upon attaining their freedom, the African states separated from the West, asserting their independence and uniqueness. This state of affairs may last beyond 1975;

yet, it is likely that before the close of the century, the African states will find their place within the changing, but essentially Western, international system and will conform more closely to Western patterns of state behavior.

It is no longer a question of *how* the international system will absorb the impact of an emerging Africa; nor even *whether* it will do so. The more relevant issue is how the new African states will adapt themselves to a changing, Western system of international political action. The consensual basis of the international system has been only temporarily disturbed by the emergence of Africa. It will reassert itself as the new African states find it necessary to conform to the Western pattern of political behavior. The international system has been affected only peripherally by an onslaught of peoples who will soon cease to appear as "intruders" to the system and will eventually take their place beside the "natives" of the system.

NOTES

1. H. L. Bretton, "The Emergence of Ghana," in A. Gyorgy and H. S. Gibb, *Problems in International Relations* (Englewood Cliffs, N.J.: Prentice-Hall, 1962), p. 238.

2. *Ibid.*

3. Rupert Emerson, "Pan-Africanism," *International Organization* Spring, 1962, p. 284.

BIBLIOGRAPHY

Du Bois, William E. B. *The World and Africa.* New York: International Publishers, 1965.

Emerson, Rupert. *Africa and United States Policy.* Englewood Cliffs, N.J.: Prentice-Hall, 1964.

Ferkiss, Victor C. *Africa's Search for Identity.* New York: George Braziller, 1966.

Goldschmidt, Walter (ed.). *The United States and Africa.* New York: Frederick A. Praeger, 1963.

HATCH, JOHN. *A History of Postwar Africa*. New York: Frederick A. Praeger, 1964.

KITCHEN, HELEN A. (ed.). *A Handbook of African Affairs*. New York: Frederick A. Praeger, 1964.

MEYER, FRANK S. *The African Nettle*. New York: The John Day Co., 1965.

PADELFORD, NORMAN J. and EMERSON, RUPERT. *Africa and World Order*. New York: Frederick A. Praeger, 1963.

RITNER, PETER. *The Death of Africa*. New York: The Macmillan Co., 1960.

RIVKIN, ARNOLD. *Africa and the West*. New York: Frederick A. Praeger, 1962.

————. *The African Presence in World Affairs*. New York: The Free Press of Glencoe, 1963.

WALLBANK, THOMAS WALTER. *Contemporary Africa*. Princeton, N.J.: Van Nostrand, 1956.

ZARTMAN, WILLIAM. *International Relations in the New Africa*. Englewood Cliffs, N.J.: Prentice-Hall, 1966.

◆ *Appendices*

APPENDIX A

VITAL STATISTICS OF THE AFRICAN STATES

Country	Date of Independence	Size (sq. mi.)	Population (000)	Capital	Head-of-State
ALGERIA	July 5, 1962	919,519	12,546	Algiers	Col. Houari Boumedienne
BOTSWANA	Sept. 30, 1966	220,000	593	Gaberones	Sir Seretse Khama
BURUNDI	July 1, 1962	11,000	3,340	Bujumbura	Col. Michel Micombero
CAMEROON	Jan. 1, 1960	184,000	470	Yaoundé	Ahmadou Ahidjo
CENTRAL AFRICAN REPUBLIC	Aug. 13, 1960	241,000	1,459	Bangui	Col. Jean B. Bokassa
CHAD	Aug. 11, 1960	496,000	3,500	Fort-Lamy	Francois Tomalbaye
CONGO (BRAZZAVILLE)	Aug. 15, 1960	132,046	860	Brazzaville	Capt. Raoul Alfred
CONGO (KINSHASA)	June 30, 1960	905,378	16,353	Kinshasa	Gen. Joseph Mobutu
DAHOMEY	Aug. 1, 1960	43,000	505	Porto Novo	Emile Derlin Zinsou
EQUATORIAL GUINEA	Oct. 12, 1968	33,047	250	Santa Isabel	Francisco Macias
ETHIOPIA	c. 1040	457,000	23,457	Addis Ababa	Haile Selassie
GABON	Aug. 17, 1960	102,000	473	Libreville	Bernard-Albert Bongo
GAMBIA	Feb. 18, 1965	4,000	343	Bathurst	David Kwesi Jawara
GHANA	March 6, 1967	92,000	8,143	Accra	Brig. Akwasi Afrifa

Country	Date of Independence	Size (sq. mi.)	Population (000)	Capital	Head-of-State
GUINEA	Oct. 2, 1958	95,000	3,702	Conakry	Ahmed Sékou Touré
IVORY COAST	Aug. 7, 1960	125,000	4,010	Abidjan	Felix Houphouet-Boigny
KENYA	Dec. 12, 1963	224,960	948	Nairobi	Jomo Kenyatta
LESOTHO	Oct. 4, 1966	12,000	885	Maseru	King Moshoeshoe II
LIBERIA	July 26, 1847	42,990	110	Monrovia	William V. S. Tubman
LIBYA	Dec. 24, 1951	679,000	738	Beida[1]	Idris al-Sanusi
MALAGASY	June 27, 1960	230,000	350	Tananarive	Philibert Tsiranana
MALAWI	July 6, 1964	46,000	4,130	Zomba[2]	Dr. H. K. Banda
MALI	Sept. 22, 1960	465,000	745	Bamako	Capt. Yoro Diakite
MAURITANIA	Nov. 28, 1960	419,000	1,110	Nouakchett	Moktar Ould Daddah
MOROCCO	March 2, 1956	187,000	14,140	Rabat	Hassan II
NIGER	Aug. 3, 1960	489,000	546	Niamey	Hamani Diori
NIGERIA	Oct. 1, 1960	357,000	61,450	Lagos	Maj. Gen. Yakubutu Gowon
RHODESIA	Nov. 17, 1965	150,333	4,530	Salisbury	Ian D. Smith[3]
RWANDA	July 1, 1962	10,169	306	Kigali	Grégoire Kayibanda
SENEGAL	Aug. 20, 1960	76,084	670	Dakar	Leopold Sedar Senghor

[1] The Libyan Constitution provides for the dual capital of Tripoli and Benghazi; however, the government is building a new capital in Beida.

[2] Zomba is the political capital; however, the foreign embassies are located in Blantyre, which is the operational capital.

[3] Clifford Dupont is representative of the Queen.

Country	Date of Independence	Size (sq. mi.)	Population (000)	Capital	Head-of-State
SIERRA LEONE	April 27, 1961	27,924	2,437	Freetown	Siaka Stevens
SOMALIA	July 1, 1960	246,000	2,666	Mogadiscio	Abdirascid Ali Scermarche
SOUTH AFRICA	May 31, 1910	472,685	18,733	Capetown	Balthazar J. Vorster
SUDAN	Jan. 1, 1956	967,498	14,355	Khartoum	Ismail El Azhari
SWAZILAND	Sept. 6, 1968	6,704	385	Mbabane	King Sobhuza
TANZANIA	Dec. 9, 1961	363,708	12,231	Dar es Salaam	Julius K. Nyerere
TOGO	April 27, 1960	22,000	1,724	Lomé	Gen. Etienne Eyadema
TUNISIA	March 20, 1956	63,078	4,560	Tunis	Habib Bourguiba
UGANDA	Oct. 9, 1962	91,000	7,934	Kampala	Milton Obote
UNITED ARAB REPUBLIC	Feb. 28, 1922	387,000	30,907	Cairo	Gamal Abdel Nasser
UPPER VOLTA	Aug. 5, 1960	106,000	5,054	Ouagadougou	Lt. Col. Sangoulé Lamizana
ZAMBIA	Oct. 24, 1964	290,323	3,947	Lusaka	Kenneth Kaunda

APPENDIX B

AFRICAN MEMBERSHIP IN PRINCIPAL REGIONAL AND INTERNATIONAL ORGANIZATIONS AND CONFERENCES

	United Nations	Organization of African Unity (OAU)	Organisation Commune Africaine et Malgache (OCAM)	Banque Africaine de Développement	Union Africaine et Malgache des Postes et Télécommunications	EEC Associates	Commonwealth	French Community	League of Arab States	Union Monétaire Ouest Africaine	Union Douanière des Etats de L'Africaine Central	Conseil de l'Entente	Monrovia Group	Brazzaville Group	Belgrade Conference	Bandung Conference	Casablanca Powers	East African Common Services Organization
ALGERIA	X	X		X					X						X		X	
BOTSWANA	X	X					X											
BURUNDI	X	X																
CAMEROON	X	X	X	X	X	X					X		X	X				
CENTRAL AFRICAN REPUBLIC	X	X	X	X	X	X		X			X		X	X				
CHAD	X	X	X		X	X		X			X		X	X				
CONGO (BRAZZAVILLE)	X	X	X	X	X	X		X			X		X	X				
CONGO (KINSHASA)	X	X	X	X	X	X							X					
DAHOMEY	X	X	X	X	X	X				X		X	X	X				
EQUATORIAL GUINEA	X																	
ETHIOPIA	X	X		X									X					
GABON	X	X	X	X	X	X		X			X		X	X	X	X		
GAMBIA	X	X					X								X	X1		

	United Nations	Organization of African Unity (OAU)	Organisation Commune Africaine et Malgache (OCAM)	Banque Africaine de Développement	Union Africaine et Malgache des Postes et Télécommunications	EEC Associates	Commonwealth	French Community	League of Arab States	Union Monétaire Ouest Africaine	Union Douanière des Etats de L'Africaine Central	Conseil de l'Entente	Monrovia Group	Brazzaville Group	Belgrade Conference	Bandung Conference	Casablanca Powers	East African Common Services Organization
GHANA	X	X		X			X								X	X	X	
GUINEA	X	X		X											X	X	X	
IVORY COAST	X	X	X	X	X	X				X		X	X	X				
KENYA	X	X		X			X						X					X
LESOTHO	X	X					X											
LIBERIA	X	X		X									X			X		
LIBYA	X	X							X				X			X		
MALAGASY	X	X	X	X	X	X		X					X	X				
MALAWI	X	X					X											
MALI	X	X				X												
MAURITANIA	X	X		X	X	X				X			X	X		X	X	
MOROCCO	X	X	X	X					X						X		X	
NIGER	X	X		X	X	X				X		X	X	X				
NIGERIA	X	X		X		X	X						X					
RHODESIA							X²											

² Rhodesia has not officially withdrawn from the Commonwealth.

	United Nations	Organization of African Unity (OAU)	Organisation Commune Africaine et Malgache (OCAM)	Banque Africaine de Développement	Union Africaine et Malgache des Postes et Télécommunications	EEC Associates	Commonwealth	French Community	League of Arab States	Union Monétaire Ouest Africaine	Union Douanière des Etats de L'Africaine Central	Conseil de l'Entente	Monrovia Group	Brazzaville Group	Belgrade Conference	Bandung Conference	Casablanca Powers	East African Common Services Organization
RWANDA	X	X	X	X	X	X												
SENEGAL	X	X	X	X	X	X		X		X			X	X				
SIERRA LEONE	X	X		X			X						X					
SOMALIA	X	X		X		X							X		X			
SOUTH AFRICA	X																	
SUDAN	X	X		X					X						X	X		
TANZANIA	X	X		X			X									X		X
TOGO	X	X	X	X	X					X		X	X					
TUNISIA	X	X		X					X				X			X		
UGANDA	X	X		X			X									X		X
UNITED ARAB REPUBLIC	X	X		X					X						X		X	
UPPER VOLTA	X	X	X	X	X	X				X		X						
ZAMBIA	X	X		X			X											

APPENDIX C

CHARTER OF THE ORGANIZATION OF AFRICAN UNITY

We, the Heads of African States and Governments assembled in the city of Addis Ababa, Ethiopia;

CONVINCED that it is the inalienable right of all people to control their own destiny;

CONSCIOUS of the fact that freedom, equality, justice and dignity are essential objectives for the achievement of the legitimate aspirations of the African peoples;

CONSCIOUS of our responsibility to harness the natural and human resources of our continent for the total advancement of our peoples in spheres of human endeavor;

INSPIRED by a common determination to strengthen understanding and cooperation among our states in response to the aspirations of our peoples for brotherhood and solidarity, in a larger unity transcending ethnic and national differences;

CONVINCED that, in order to translate this determination into a dynamic force in the cause of human progress, conditions for peace and security must be established and maintained;

DETERMINED to consolidate and safeguard the hard-won independence as well as sovereignty and territorial integrity of our states, and to fight against neo-colonialism in all its forms;

DEDICATED to the general progress of Africa;

PERSUADED that the Charter of the United Nations and the Universal Declaration of Human Rights, to the principles of which we reaffirm our adherence, provide a solid foundation for peaceful and positive cooperation among states;

DESIROUS that all African states should henceforth unite so that the welfare and well-being of their peoples can be assured;

RESOLVED to reinforce the links between our states by establishing and strengthening common institutions;

HAVE agreed to the present Charter.

Establishment

Article I

(1) The High Contracting Parties do by the present Charter establish an organization to be known as the "Organization of African Unity."

(2) The organization shall include the continental African states, Madagascar, and other islands surrounding Africa.

Purposes

Article II

(1) The organization shall have the following purposes: (a) to promote the unity and solidarity of the African states; (b) to coordinate and intensify their cooperation and efforts to achieve a better life for the peoples of Africa; (c) to defend their sovereignty, their territorial integrity, and independence; (d) to eradicate all forms of colonialism from Africa; and (e) to promote international cooperation, having due regard to the Charter of the United Nations and the Universal Declaration of Human Rights.

(2) To these ends, the member states shall coordinate and harmonize their general policies, especially in the following fields: (a) political and diplomatic cooperation; (b) economic cooperation, including transport and communications; (c) educational and cultural cooperation; (d) health, sanitation, and nutritional cooperation; (e) scientific and technical cooperation; and (f) cooperation for defense and security.

Principles

Article III

The member states, in pursuit of the purposes stated in Article II, solemnly affirm and declare their adherence to the following principles:

(1) the sovereign equality of all member states;

(2) non-interference in the internal affairs of states;

(3) respect for the sovereignty and territorial integrity of each member state and for its inalienable right to independent existence;

(4) peaceful settlement of disputes by negotiation, mediation, conciliation or arbitration;

(5) unreserved condemnation, in all its forms, of political assassination as well as of subversive activities on the part of neighboring states or any other states;

(6) absolute dedication to the total emancipation of the African territories which are still dependent;

(7) affirmation of a policy of non-alignment with regard to all blocs.

Membership

Article IV

Each independent sovereign African state shall be entitled to become a member of the organization.

Rights and Duties of Member States

Article V

All member states shall enjoy equal rights and have equal duties.

Article VI

The member states pledge themselves to observe scrupulously the principles enumerated in Article III of the present Charter.

Institutions

Article VII

The organization shall accomplish its purposes through the following principal institutions:

(1) the Assembly of Heads of State and Government;

(2) the Council of Ministers;

(3) the General Secretariat;
(4) the Commission of Mediation, Conciliation, and Arbitration.

The Assembly of Heads of State and Government

Article VIII

The Assembly of Heads of State and Government shall be the supreme organ of the organization. It shall, subject to the provisions of this Charter, discuss matters of common concern to Africa with a view to coordinating and harmonizing the general policy of the organization. It may, in addition, review the structure, functions, and acts of all the organs and any specialized agencies which may be created in accordance with the present Charter.

Article IX

The Assembly shall be composed of the Heads of State and Government, or their duly accredited representatives, and it shall meet at least once a year. At the request of any member state, and on approval by a two-thirds majority of the member states, the Assembly shall meet in extraordinary session.

Article X

(1) Each member state shall have one vote.
(2) All resolutions shall be determined by a two-thirds majority of the members of the organization.
(3) Questions of procedure shall require a simple majority. Whether or not a question is one of procedure shall be determined by a simple majority of all member states of the organization.
(4) Two-thirds of the total membership of the organization shall form a quorum at any meeting of the Assembly.

Article XI

The Assembly shall have the power to determine its own rules of procedure.

The Council of Ministers

Article XII

The Council of Ministers shall consist of Foreign Ministers or such other Ministers as are designated by the Governments of member states.

The Council of Ministers shall meet at least twice a year. When requested by any member state and approved by two-thirds of all member states, it shall meet in extraordinary session.

Article XIII

The Council of Ministers shall be responsible to the Assembly of Heads of State and Government. It shall be entrusted with the responsibility of preparing conferences of the Assembly.

It shall take cognizance of any matter referred to it by the Assembly. It shall be entrusted with the implementation of the decisions of the Assembly of Heads of State and Government. It shall coordinate inter-African cooperation in accordance with the instructions of the Assembly and in conformity with Article II (2) of the present Charter.

Article XIV

(1) Each member state shall have one vote.

(2) All resolutions shall be determined by a simple majority of the Council Ministers.

(3) Two-thirds of the total membership of the Council shall form a quorum for any meeting of the Council.

Article XV

The Council shall have the power to determine its own rules of procedure.

General Secretariat

Article XVI

There shall be an Administrative Secretary-General of the organization, who shall be appointed by the Assembly of Heads of State and Government, on the recommendation of the Council of Ministers. The administrative Secretary-General shall direct the affairs of the Secretariat.

Article XVII

There shall be one or more Assistant Secretaries-General of the organization, who shall be appointed by the Assembly of Heads of State and Government.

Article XVIII

The functions and conditions of service of the Secretary-General, of the Assistant Secretaries-General, and other employees of the Secretariat shall be governed by the provisions of this Charter and the regulations approved by the Assembly of Heads of State and Government.

(1) In the performance of their duties the Administrative Secretary-General and the staff shall not seek or receive instructions from any government or from any other authority external to the organization. They shall refrain from any action which might reflect on their position as international officials responsible only to the organization.

(2) Each member of the organization undertakes to respect the exclusive character of the responsibilities of the Administrative Secretary-General and the staff and not to seek to influence them in the discharge of their responsibilities.

Commission of Mediation, Conciliation, and Arbitration

Article XIX

Member states pledge to settle all disputes among themselves by peaceful means and, to this end, decide to establish a Commission of Mediation, Conciliation, and Arbitration, the composition of which and conditions of service shall be defined by a separate protocol to be approved by the Assembly of Heads of State and Government. Said protocol shall be regarded as forming an integral part of the present Charter.

Specialized Commissions

Article XX

The Assembly shall establish such Specialized Commissions as it may deem necessary, including the following:

(1) Economic and Social Commission;
(2) Educational and Cultural Commission;
(3) Health, Sanitation, and Nutrition Commission;
(4) Defence Commission;
(5) Scientific, Technical, and Research Commission.

Article XXI

Each Specialized Commission referred to in Article XX shall be composed of the Ministers concerned or other Ministers or Plenipotentiaries designated by the Governments of the member states.

Article XXII

The functions of the Specialized Commissions shall be carried out in accordance with the provisions of the present Charter and of the regulations approved by the Council of Ministers.

The Budget

Article XXIII

The budget of the organization prepared by the Administrative Secretary-General shall be approved by the Council of Ministers. The budget shall be provided by contributions from member states in accordance with the scale of assessment of the United Nations; provided, however, that no member state shall be assessed an amount exceeding twenty percent of the yearly regular budget of the organization. The member states agree to pay their respective contributions regularly.

Signature and Ratification of Charter

Article XXIV

This Charter shall be open for signature to all independent sovereign African states and shall be ratified by the signatory states in accordance with their respective constitutional processes.

The original instrument, done, if possible, in African languages, in English and French, all texts being equally authentic, shall be deposited with the Government of Ethiopia, which shall transmit certified copies thereof to all independent sovereign African states. Instruments of ratification shall be deposited with the Government of Ethiopia, which shall notify all signatories of each such deposit.

Entry into Force

Article XXV

This Charter shall enter into force immediately upon receipt by the Government of Ethiopia of the instruments of ratification from two-thirds of the signatory states.

Registration of the Charter

Article XXVI

This Charter shall, after due ratification, be registered with the Secretariat of the United Nations through the Government of Ethiopia in conformity with Article 102 of the Charter of the United Nations.

Interpretation of the Charter

Article XXVII

Any question which may arise concerning the interpretation of this Charter shall be decided by a vote of two-thirds of the Assembly of Heads of State and Government of the organization.

Adhesion and Accession

Article XXVIII

(1) Any independent sovereign African State may at any time notify the Administrative Secretary-General of its intention to adhere or accede to this Charter.

(2) The Administrative Secretary-General shall, on receipt of such notification, communicate a copy of it to all the member

states. Admission shall be decided by a simple majority of member states. The decision of each member state shall be transmitted to the Administrative Secretary-General, who shall, upon receipt of the required number of votes, communicate the decision to the state concerned.

Miscellaneous

Article XXIX

The working languages of the organization and all its institutions shall be, if possible, African languages, English and French.

Article XXX

The Administrative Secretary-General may accept on behalf of the organization gifts, bequests, and other donations made to the organization, provided that this is approved by the Council of Ministers.

Article XXXI

The Council of Ministers shall decide on the privileges and immunities to be accorded to the personnel of the Secretariat in the respective territories of the member states.

Cessation of Membership

Article XXXII

Any state which desires to renounce its membership shall forward a written notification to the Administrative Secretary-General. At the end of one year from the date of such notification, if not withdrawn, the Charter shall cease to apply with respect to the renouncing state, which shall thereby cease to belong to the organization.

Amendment of the Charter

Article XXXIII

This Charter may be amended or revised if any member state makes a written request to the Administrative Secretary-

General to that effect, provided, however, that the proposed amendment is not submitted to the Assembly for consideration until all the member states have been duly notified of it and a period of one year has elapsed. Such an amendment shall not be effective unless approved by at least two-thirds of all the member states.

Members

Algeria	Malawi
Burundi	Mali
Cameroon	Mauritania
Central African Republic	Morocco
Chad	Niger
Congo (Brazzaville)	Nigeria
Congo (Leopoldville)	Rwanda
Dahomey	Senegal
Ethiopia	Somalia
Gabon	Sierra Leone
Gambia	Sudan
Ghana	Togo
Guinea	Tunisia
Ivory Coast	Uganda
Kenya	United Arab Republic
Liberia	United Republic of Tanzania
Libya	Upper Volta
Madagascar	Zambia

APPENDIX D

FINAL COMMUNIQUE OF THE ASIAN-AFRICAN CONFERENCE, BANDUNG, APRIL 24, 1955

The Asian-African Conference, convened upon the invitation of the Prime Ministers of Burma, Ceylon, India, Indonesia and Pakistan, met in Bandung from the 18th to the 24th April, 1955. In addition to the sponsoring countries the following 24 countries participated in the conference:

1. Afghanistan
2. Cambodia
3. People's Republic of China
4. Egypt
5. Ethiopia
6. Gold Coast
7. Iran
8. Iraq
9. Japan
10. Jordan
11. Laos
12. Lebanon
13. Liberia
14. Libya
15. Nepal
16. Philippines
17. Saudi Arabia
18. Sudan
19. Syria
20. Thailand
21. Turkey
22. Democratic Republic of Vietnam
23. State of Vietnam
24. Yemen

The Asian-African Conference considered problems of common interest and concern to countries of Asia and Africa and discussed ways and means by which their people could achieve fuller economic, cultural and political cooperation.

A. Economic Cooperation

1. The Asian-African Conference recognized the urgency of promoting economic development in the Asian-African region. There was general desire for economic cooperation among the participating countries on the basis of mutual interest and respect for national sovereignty. The proposals with regard to economic cooperation within the participating countries do not preclude either the desirability or the need for cooperation with countries outside the region, including the investment of foreign capital. It was further recognized that the assistance being received by certain participating countries from outside the region, through international or under bilateral arrangements, had made a valuable contribution to the implementation of their development programmes.

2. The participating countries agreed to provide technical assistance to one another, to the maximum extent practicable, in the form of: experts, trainees, pilot projects and equipment for demonstration purposes; exchange of know-how and establishment of national, and where possible, regional training and research institutes for imparting technical knowledge and skills in cooperation with the existing international agencies.

3. The Asian-African Conference recommended: the early establishment of the Special United Nations Fund for Economic Development; the allocation by the International Bank for Reconstruction and Development of a greater part of its resources to Asian-African countries; the early establishment of the International Finance Corporation which should include in its activities the undertaking of equity investment, and encouragement to the promotion of joint ventures among Asian-African countries in so far as this will promote their common interest.

4. The Asian-African Conference recognized the vital need for stabilizing commodity trade in the region. The principle of enlarging the scope of multilateral trade and payments was accepted. However, it was recognized that some countries would have to take recourse to bilateral trade arrangements in view of their prevailing economic conditions.

5. The Asian-African Conference recommended that collective action be taken by participating countries for stabilizing the international prices of and demand for primary commodities through bilateral and multilateral arrangements, and that as far as practicable and desirable, they should adopt a unified approach on the subject in the United Nations Permanent Advisory Commission on International Commodity Trade and other international forums.

6. The Asian-African Conference further recommended that: Asian-African countries should diversify their export trade by processing their raw material, wherever economically feasible, before export; intraregional trade fairs should be promoted and encouragement given to the exchange of trade delegations and groups of businessmen; exchange of information and of samples should be encouraged with a view to promoting intra-regional trade and normal facilities should be provided for transit trade of land-locked countries.

7. The Asian-African Conference attached considerable importance to Shipping and expressed concern that shipping lines reviewed from time to time their freight rates, often to the detriment of participating countries. It recommended a study of this problem, and collective action thereafter, to induce the shipping lines to adopt a more reasonable attitude. It was suggested that a study of railway freight of transit trade may be made.

8. The Asian-African Conference agreed that encouragement should be given to the establishment of national and regional banks and insurance companies.

9. The Asian-African Conference felt that exchange of information on matters relating to oil, such as remittance of profits and taxation, might eventually lead to the formulation of common policies.

10. The Asian-African Conference emphasized the particular significance of the development of nuclear energy for peaceful purposes, for the Asian-African countries. The Conference welcomed the initiative of the Powers principally concerned in offering to make available information regarding the use of atomic energy for peaceful purposes; urged the speedy establishment of the International Atomic Energy Agency which should provide for adequate representation of the Asian-African countries on the executive authority of the Agency; and recommended to the Asian and African Governments to take full advantage of the training and other facilities in the peaceful uses of atomic energy offered by the countries sponsoring such programmes.

11. The Asian-African Conference agreed to the appointment of Liaison Officers in participating countries, to be nominated by their respective national Governments, for the exchange of information and ideas on matters of mutual interest. It recommended that fuller use should be made of the existing international organizations, and participating countries who were not members of such international organizations, but were eligible, should secure membership.

12. The Asian-African Conference recommended that there should be prior consultation of participating countries in international forums with a view, as far as possible, to furthering their mutual economic interest. It is, however, not intended to form a regional bloc.

B. Cultural Cooperation

1. The Asian-African Conference was convinced that among the most powerful means of promoting understanding among nations is the development of cultural cooperation. Asia and Africa have been the cradle of great religions and civilizations which have enriched other cultures and civilizations while themselves being enriched in the process. Thus the cultures of Asia and Africa are based on spiritual and universal foundations. Unfortunately contacts among Asian and African countries were

interrupted during the past centuries. The peoples of Asia and Africa are now animated by a keen and sincere desire to renew the old cultural contacts and develop new ones in the context of the modern world. All participating Governments at the Conference reiterated their determination to work for closer cultural cooperation.

2. The Asian-African Conference took note of the fact that the existence of colonialism in many parts of Asia and Africa in whatever form it may be not only prevents cultural cooperation but also suppresses the national cultures of the people. Some colonial powers have denied to their dependent peoples basic rights in the sphere of education and culture which hampers the development of their personality and also prevents cultural intercourse with other Asian and African peoples. This is particularly true in the case of Tunisia, Algeria and Morocco, where the basic right of the people to study their own language and culture has been suppressed. Similar discrimination has been practised against African and coloured people in some parts of the Continent of Africa. The Conference felt that these policies amount to a denial of the fundamental rights of man, impede cultural advancement in this region and also hamper cultural cooperation on the wider international plane. The Conference condemned such a denial of fundamental rights in the sphere of education and culture in some parts of Asia and Africa by this and other forms of cultural suppression.

In particular, the Conference condemned racialism as a means of cultural suppression.

3. It was not from any sense of exclusiveness or rivalry with other groups of nations and other civilisations and cultures that the Conference viewed the development of cultural cooperation among Asian and African countries. True to the age-old tradition of tolerance and universality, the Conference believed that Asian and African cultural cooperation should be developed in the larger context of world cooperation.

Side by side with the development of Asian-African cultural cooperation the countries of Asia and Africa desire to develop cultural contacts with others. This would enrich their own culture and would also help in the promotion of world peace and understanding.

4. There are many countries in Asia and Africa which have

not been able to develop their educational, scientific and technical institutions. The Conference recommended that countries in Asia and Africa which are more fortunately placed in this respect should give facilities for the admission of students and trainees from such countries to their institutions. Such facilities should also be made available to the Asian and African people in Africa to whom opportunities for acquiring higher education are at present denied.

5. The Asian-African Conference felt that the promotion of cultural cooperation among countries of Asia and Africa should be directed towards:

(I)   the acquisition of knowledge of each other's country,
(II) mutual cultural exchange, and
(III) exchange of information.

6. The Asian-African Conference was of opinion that at this stage the best results in cultural cooperation would be achieved by pursuing bilateral arrangements to implement its recommendations and by each country taking action on its own, wherever possible and feasible.

C. Human Rights and Self-determination

1. The Asian-African Conference declared its full support of the fundamental principles of Human Rights as set forth in the Charter of the United Nations and took note of the Universal Declaration of Human Rights as a common standard of achievement for all peoples and all nations.

The Conference declared its full support of the principles of self-determination of peoples and nations as set forth in the Charter of the United Nations and took note of the United Nations resolutions on the rights of peoples and nations to self-determination, which is a pre-requisite of the full enjoyment of all fundamental Human Rights.

2. The Asian-African Conference deplored the policies and practices of racial segregation and discrimination which form the basis of government and human relations in large regions of Africa and in other parts of the world. Such conduct is not only

a gross violation of human rights, but also a denial of the fundamental values of civilisation and the dignity of man.

The Conference extended its warm sympathy and support
for the courageous stand taken by the victims of racial discrimination, especially by the peoples of African and Indian and
Pakistani origin in South Africa; applauded all those who sustain
their cause; re-affirmed the determination of Asian-African
peoples to eradicate every trace of racialism that might exist in
their own countries; and pledged to use its full moral influence to
guard against the danger of falling victims to the same evil in
their struggle to eradicate it.

D. Problems of Dependent Peoples

1. The Asian-African Conference discussed the problems of
dependent peoples and colonialism and the evils arising from the
subjection of peoples to alien subjugation, domination and
exploitation.

The Conference is agreed:

(a) in declaring that colonialism in all its manifestations is
an evil which should speedily be brought to an end;

(b) in affirming that the subjection of peoples to alien subjugation, domination and exploitation constitutes a
denial of fundamental human rights, is contrary to the
Charter of the United Nations and is an impediment to
the promotion of world peace and cooperation;

(c) in declaring its support of the cause of freedom and
independence for all such people, and

(d) in calling upon the powers concerned to grant freedom
and independence to such peoples.

2. In view of the unsettled situation in North Africa and of
the persisting denial to the peoples of North Africa of their right
to self-determination, the Asian-African Conference declared its
support of the rights of the people of Algeria, Morocco and
Tunisia to self-determination and independence and urged the
French Government to bring about a peaceful settlement of the
issue without delay.

E. Other Problems

1. In view of the existing tension in the Middle East, caused by the situation in Palestine, and of the danger of that tension to world peace, the Asian-African Conference declared its support of the rights of the Arab people of Palestine and called for the implementation of the United Nations Resolutions on Palestine and the achievement of the peaceful settlement of the Palestine question.

2. The Asian-African Conference, in the context of its expressed attitude on the abolition of colonialism, supported the position of Indonesia in the case of West Irian based on the relevant agreements between Indonesia and the Netherlands.

The Asian-African Conference urged the Netherlands Government to reopen negotiations as soon as possible, to implement their obligations under the above-mentioned agreements, and expressed the earnest hope that the United Nations would assist the parties concerned in finding a peaceful solution to the dispute.

3. The Asian-African Conference supported the position of Yemen in the case of Aden and the Southern parts of Yemen known as the Protectorates and urged the parties concerned to arrive at a peaceful settlement of the dispute.

F. Promotion of World Peace and Cooperation

1. The Asian-African Conference, taking note of the fact that several States have still not been admitted to the United Nations, considered that for effective cooperation for world peace, membership in the United Nations should be universal, called on the Security Council to support the admission of all those States which are qualified for membership in terms of the Charter. In the opinion of the Asian-African Conference, the following among participating countries, viz: Cambodia, Ceylon, Japan, Jordan, Libya, Nepal, a unified Vietnam,were so qualified.

The Conference considered that the representation of the countries of the Asian-African region on the Security Council, in relation to the principle of equitable geographical distribution, was inadequate. It expressed the view that as regards the distribution of the non-permanent seats, the Asian-African countries which, under the arrangement arrived at in London in 1946, are precluded from being elected, should be enabled to serve on the

Security Council, so that they might make a more effective contribution to the maintenance of international peace and security.

2. The Asian-African Conference having considered the dangerous situation of international tension existing and the risks confronting the whole human race from the outbreak of global war in which the destructive power of all types of armaments, including nuclear and thermo-nuclear weapons, would be employed, invited the attention of all nations to the terrible consequences that would follow if such a war were to break out.

The Conference considered that disarmament and the prohibition of the production, experimentation and use of nuclear and thermo-nuclear weapons of war are imperative to save mankind and civilization from the fear and prospect of wholesale destruction. It considered that the nations of Asia and Africa assembled here have a duty towards humanity and civilization to proclaim their support for disarmament and for the prohibition of these weapons and to appeal to nations principally concerned and to world opinion, to bring about such disarmament and prohibition.

The Conference considered that effective international control should be established and maintained to implement such disarmament and prohibition and that speedy and determined efforts should be made to this end.

Pending the total prohibition of the manufacture of nuclear and thermo-nuclear weapons, this Conference appealed to all the powers concerned to reach agreement to suspend experiments with such weapons.

The Conference declared that universal disarmament is an absolute necessity for the preservation of peace and requested the United Nations to continue its efforts and appealed to all concerned speedily to bring about the regulation, limitation, control and reduction of all armed forces and armaments, including the prohibition of the production, experimentation and use of all weapons of mass destruction, and to establish effective international control to this end.

G. Declaration on the Promotion of World Peace and Cooperation

The Asian-African Conference gave anxious thought to the question of world peace and cooperation. It viewed with deep concern the present state of international tension with its danger of an atomic world war. The problem of peace is correlative with the problem of international security. In this connection, all States should cooperate, especially through the United Nations, in bringing about the reduction of armaments and the elimination of nuclear weapons under effective international control. In this way, international peace can be promoted and nuclear energy may be used exclusively for peaceful purposes. This would help answer the needs particularly of Asia and Africa, for what they urgently require are social progress and better standards of life in larger freedom. Freedom and peace are interdependent. The right of self-determination must be enjoyed by all peoples, and freedom and independence must be granted, with the least possible delay, to those who are still dependent peoples. Indeed, all nations should have the right freely to choose their own political and economic systems and their own way of life, in conformity with the purposes and principles of the Charter of the United Nations.

Free from mistrust and fear, and with confidence and goodwill towards each other, nations should practise tolerance and live together in peace with one another as good neighbours and develop friendly cooperation on the basis of the following principles:

1. Respect for fundamental human rights and for the purposes and principles of the Charter of the United Nations.
2. Respect for the sovereignty and territorial integrity of all nations.
3. Recognition of the equality of all races and of the equality of all nations large and small.
4. Abstention from intervention or interference in the internal affairs of another country.
5. Respect for the right of each nation to defend itself singly or collectively, in conformity with the Charter of the United Nations.
6. (a) Abstention from the use of arrangements of collective defense to serve the particular interests of any of the big powers.
   (b) Abstention by any country from exerting pressures on other countries.

7. Refraining from acts or threats of aggression or the use of force against the territorial integrity or political independence of any country.
8. Settlement of all international disputes by peaceful means, such as negotiation, conciliation, arbitration or judicial settlement as well as other peaceful means of the parties' own choice, in conformity with the Charter of the United Nations.
9. Promotion of mutual interests and cooperation.
10. Respect for justice and international obligations.

The Asian-African Conference declared its conviction that friendly cooperation in accordance with these principles would effectively contribute to the maintenance and promotion of international peace and security, while cooperation in the economic, social and cultural fields would help bring about the common prosperity and well-being of all.

The Asian-African Conference recommended that the five sponsoring countries consider the convening of the next meeting of the Conference, in consultation with the participating countries.

Bandung, 24th April, 1955

*Survey of International Affairs, 1955-56 (London: Oxford University Press, 1960), pp. 57-65.

◆ *Index*

AAPO, 115, 117

Accra, 23, 114, 115

Addis Ababa Conference, 118, 120

Africa (*see also* African states, Non-West):
  bridge between West and non-West, 109
  facing Western culture, 20-22, 39-40, 43
  impact of change on, 19-20
  political literature on, 1-2, 3
  position in international system, 129-142, 144-158
  recent studies on, 2-8
  revolutionary thought in, 47-67

"Africa for Africans," principle of nationalist programs, 113

African Consultative Assembly, 117

African elites (*see also* African leaders):
  alienated, 39, 86
  military as leaders, 41-42
  searching for principles, 72
  tasks of, 39
  three types of, 135-136
  and Western culture, 7, 20

African federalism (*see* Federalism)

African foreign policy, 136

African goals, ill-defined, 40

African identity, 10, 104, 129, 134, 136

African image of international politics, 129-132

African leaders (*see also* African elites):

African leaders *(Cont.)*
  challenged, 40-41
  conversant with Western political ideas, 43
  deal with both blocs, 27, 135
  desire to develop ideology and development of new states, 9, 123, 150
  embodiment of new states, 61-62
  inadequately prepared, 39-40
  and Pan-Africanism, 108-109, 122, 124
  power concentrated in, 61-65
  relation to tribe, 30
  sovereign leaders, 134

African nationalism (*see* Nationalism)

African personality, 36, 83, 85, 113, 122, 150

African socialism (*see* Socialism)

African states
  army in, 41
  boundaries reflect absurdities, 26
  composition, 70
  domestic political environment, 61
  factor in international politics, 1, 9, 120, 129, 142
  goals, 40, 135
  independent by default, 16
  lack national solidarity, 9
  national progress measure of development, 35-36
  objective, 44
  regional arrangements, 124

African states *(Cont.)*
  relation to Soviet Union, 27,
    105, 130
  threatened from within and
    without, 123
  underdeveloped by Western
    standards, 2
  and United States, 148
African system, 150-156
African thought, revolutionary,
    47-67
Afro-Asian bloc, a myth, 137-139
Afro-Malagasy Economic Cooperation
    Organization (AMEC), 116
Aid accepted from all sources,
    26-27, 131, 134, 135 (*see also*
    Foreign aid)
Algeria, 18, 25, 42, 49, 117, 152
All-Africa Peoples Organization,
    115, 117
AMEC, 116
Anthropologists and analyses of
    non-West, 2, 5
Anti-colonialism, 72-75
  attitude of intellectuals
    toward, 27
  comprehensive, 134
  a major issue, 62
  nationalist goal, 39, 83,
    113, 114, 146-147
  target of revolutionary thought,
    66
April Conference of Eight Inde-
    pendent States of Africa, 114
Arab socialist movement, 100-103
Arab Socialist Union, 102
Army function in African states, 41
Assimilation, policy of colonialism,
    38-39
Association, policy of colonialism,
    38-39
Aswan Dam, 102
Atlantic Charter, 112
Authoritarianism in African leaders,
    40, 61-65
Azikiwe, Nnamdi, 112

Balewa, 117
Bandung Conference, 101, 138, 180

Basutoland, 118
Bechuanaland, 118
Behavioral approach to political
    development study, 4-8
Belgian colonial policy, 37
Ben Bella, Ahmed, 42
Bipolar international system, 16,
    19, 129
Black Africa, concept of Senghor, 83
Black Culture, 53
Boumedienne, Houari, 152
Bourguiba, Habib, 49, 152
  and nationalism, 79-80
  and revolutionary thought, 57-58
  and socialism, 103
British colonial policy, 36-37

Cameroons, 111, 112, 151
Capitalism:
  in current African thought, 48
  foreign to African traditions,
    104
  a means of change, 105
Casablanca Conference, 117, 164-166
Change:
  by communism or socialism, as
    opposed to capitalism, 105
  effect on Africa, 19-22
  problems of, 29-44
  since Second World War, 1, 16,
    18-19
Chinese aid, 27
Christianity in Africa, 32-35
  as a symbol, 35
  and tribal institutions, 36
Cold war, 3, 27, 128, 131
  effect on West, 138
  future, 141
  vital to African independence,
    128-130
Colonial policy, 1, 2
  Belgian, 37
  British, 36-37
  French, 37-38
  Portuguese, 37-38
Colonialism (*see also* Anti-
    colonialism, Neo-colonialism,
    Residual colonialism):
  according to Fanon, 50

Colonialism *(Cont.)*
the common enemy, 136
current African concept, 130
denied racial equality, 73
early, 17-18
legacy of, 35-39
Committee on Comparative Politics
of Social Science Research
Council, 5
Common heritage, questionable
basis for unity, 109
Communalism, 113
Communism:
African view of, 130
a means of change, 105
Communist aid, influence questionable, 27
Communist models, adapted by
non-West, 105-106
Congresses, international Pan-
African, 111-113
Consciencism, 54
Conseil de l'Entente, 116, 164-166
Consensus, 63
absence in new African states, 48
in democracy, 43
factor in behavioral studies, 8
and Maliki doctrine, 34
organized by nationalism, 69
policy of Nyerere, 58-59
Continuity, problems of, 29-45
Convention Peoples' Party (CPP),
42, 113
Cooperative ventures, 104
CPP, 113

Dahomey, 116
December All-African Peoples
Conference, 114-115
Democracy:
with Arab socialism, 103
betrayed to special interests, 48
and political development, 6-7
principle of nationalist programs, 113, 115
successful functioning of, 43
Destourian socialism, 103
Destourian Socialist Party, 58, 79
Dia, Mamadou, 44

Disillusionment after independence,
48
Divisive effects in building new
state, 9
Dual mandate system, 36-37
DuBois, W. E. B., 36-37

EACSO, 119, 164-166
Early analyses of non-West, 2
East African Common Service Organization (EACSO), 119
East African Development Bank, 119
East African High Commission, 119
Economic development:
of non-West, 4, 91-92, 94-96,
98-99, 102-106, 148-149
relation to political, 3, 5
role of African government in,
104
Economists, and study of political
development, 5
EEC, 116, 122, 164-166
Egalitarianism, factor in
socialism, 92-93, 95
Egypt *(see also* Nasser):
dispute with Sudan, 153
link between Africa and outside,
56
relation to Arabs, 78-79
relation to Britain, 77-78
relation to China, 27
relation to India, 27
revolutions proposed by Nasser,
55-57
and socialist neutralism,
101-102
Elites *(see* African elites,
African leaders)
Ethiopia, 32, 138, 152
European Economic Community
(EEC), 116, 122

Fanon, Frantz, 48-53
exponent of African revolutionary
thought, 49
philosophy of, 49-53
Federalism:
explored by AAPO, 115

Federalism *(Cont.)*
  and OAU, 120, 121
  principle of nationalist
    programs, 113
FLN, 42, 49, 117
Forces of change, 17-19
Foreign aid:
  and change in approach to
    African studies, 4
  consequence of, 55
  medium of political pressure, 25
Freedom, sought through nationalism,
  10, 66, 69-87
Future of international system,
  156-158

Gandhi's non-violence a model,
  112, 114
Gap between old and new, 9
Ghana, 42, 53, 112, 117, 122, 138,
  151, 153
  joined with Guinea, 115
  joined with Guinea and Mali, 116
  problems of reconstruction,
    75-77, 99-100
Gold Coast (*see* Ghana)
Gold Coast Trade Union Congress, 113
Great power rivalry, 27
Guinea, 59-60, 115, 116, 117

Hassan, 27, 152
Houphouet-Boigny, Felix, 49, 60-61,
  116, 151
  belief in absolute neutrality, 61
  and Pan-Africanism, 61

Identity, national, 10, 104, 129,
  134, 136
Imperialism, preoccupying elites, 6
Increasing role of non-West, 23
Independence:
  conception of, 71-72
  and responsibilities, 30
Individual freedom lacking in
  tribal organization, 30
Interdependence a fact, 140, 147-148
International Co-operation Adminis-
  tration, 3

International political system:
  Africa's effect on, 144-158
  Africa's image of, 128-132
  changed by numerous new states,
    144-145
  effect on Africa, 15-27
  forces of change, 17-19
  increasingly interwoven, 16-17,
    22-27
  non-alignment and, 132-142
Irredentism, 151-152
Islam, 31-35
  effect on today's problems, 29
  heterogeneity of, 34
  influence on socialism, 102, 103
  instrument of authority, 34
  legacy, 100
Israel, 154
Ivory Coast, 60-61, 116, 151

KANU, 81
Kenya, 80-82, 118, 152
Kenya African National Union
  (KANU), 81
Kenyatta, Jomo, 49
  EACSO treaty, 119
  and nationalism, 80-82
  PAFMECSA, 118
  and socialism, 93-95

League of Nations, 111
Liberalism:
  sacrificed in Africa, 106
  seen no menace, 130
  in social thought in Africa, 48

Maghrebian unity, 80, 152
Mali, 116, 117
Mali Federation, 116
Maliki doctrine, 34
Marxism:
  incompatible with liberalism, 16,
    106
  as means of progress distinct
    from ideology, 105
Mau-Mau, 81
Mauritania, 26, 117, 152
Mboya, Tom, 114-115, 118

Mediator function of Africa:
  basic tenet of leaders, 131, 137
  lessening, 139
Minority participation, overlooked, 63
"Modern" state, 8-9
Modernization:
  African efforts diverse, 155
  distinct from Westernization, 148-149
  a force of cohesion, 149
  goal, 135
  issues, 1, 3
  ostentatious in new Africa, 62, 148-149
  political socialization the key to, 5
Monrovia Conference, 117-118, 120
Monrovia group, 121, 164-166
Morocco, 26, 27, 117, 152
Multi-racial goal, 115
Muslim culture, 57
Muslims:
  adherents of Islam, 31-34
  not a homogeneous group, 34

Nasser, Gamal Abdel, 55-57, 58, 80, 130
  allows no Communist party in Egypt, 57
  on democracy in Egypt, 56-57
  and nationalism, 77-79
  and Pan-Arabism, 78-79
  on revolutionary thought, 55-57
  and socialism, 48, 100-103
  sponsor of Afro-Asian bloc, 138
Nation-state concept, 20, 86
  changed, 15
  continued in Africa today, 154-155
  goal of nationalists, 70-71
  and socialism, 92
National Council of Nigeria and the Cameroons (NCNC), 112-113
National Liberation Front (FLN), 42, 49, 117
Nationalism, 69-87, 146, 150
  assessment, 83-87
  created by impact of West, 43, 70
  factor in pursuit of freedom, 10, 66, 69-87

Nationalism (Cont.)
  goal, 70-71
  tribe a rallying point for, 30
Native philosophy, according to Fanon, 50
NCNC, 112
Negritude, 73, 85, 150
  concept of Senghor, 44, 83
  definition, 109
Nehru:
  conceived strategy of non-alignment, 138
  offered aid by Egypt, 27
Neo-colonialism, 6, 74-75, 78, 124
  preoccupying elites, 66
  refashioned anti-colonialism, 146-148
  threat to African existence, 55, 129
Neo-Destourian Party, 79
Neutralism (see also Non-alignment):
  of African governments, 101, 103
  for Arab world, 101
  factor in security, 10, 67, 128-142
  meaning non-alignment, 128
  and neutrality, 67
  a prestige factor, 149
  proposed by socialists, 101
Neutrality:
  definition, 132-133
  and non-alignment, 132-133
  a policy of Houphouet-Boigny, 13, 61
Niger, 116
Nigeria, 112, 113, 122, 150, 151
Nkrumah, Kwame, 53-55, 108, 151
  and authoritarian socialism, 94, 98-100
  consciencism, 54
  eliminated by coup, 42
  exponent of unity, 121
  and Kenyatta, 81
  and OAU, 120
  and Pan-Africanism, 54-55, 77, 122, 125
  philosophy of African revolution, 53-55
  plan for national liberation, 75-77

Nkrumah, Kwame *(Cont.)*
    and rise of nationalist group,
        112-116
    sponsor of Afro-Asian bloc, 138
Non-alignment *(see also* Neutralism):
    advocated by Nasser, 55
    allows fluid system, 131
    assessment, 139-142
    conceived by Nehru, 138
    danger of, for African states,
        142
    functions, 132-137
    meaning neutralism, 128
    opposed to neutrality, 133
    possible with African unity,
        108-109
    practical benefits, 128, 135-137
    principle of nationalist
        programs, 114
    response to contemporary
        conditions, 128
    socialism compatible with, 93
Non-West *(see also* Africa, African
    states):
    borrowing from East and West, 106
    definition, 1
    early transition period, 2-6
    factor in international politics, 1,
        9, 29, 142, 144-158
Nuclear warfare, 16, 131
Nyasaland, 118, 151-152
Nyerere, Julius, 48, 130, 152
    and capitalism, 44
    and democratic socialism, 94
    EACSO treaty, 119
    PAFMECSA, 118
    on revolutionary thought, 58-59

OAU *(see* Organization of African
    Unity)
Obote, Milton, 119
Olympio, 117, 151
One-party control, 61-65, 87
Order, secured through Pan-
    Africanism, 10, 66
Organization of African Unity (OAU),
    118, 120-122, 123, 164-166
    charter, 120, 167
    and federalism, 123-124

Organization of African Unity *(Cont.)*
    radical and moderate groups,
        121-122

PAFMECSA, 118, 121, 152
Pan-African congresses (1919-1945),
    111-113
Pan-African Federation, 112
Pan-African Freedom Movement for
    East, Central, and South Africa
    (PAFMECSA), 118, 121, 152
Pan-Africanism:
    agreement difficult, 123
    aims, 108, 109, 110
    assessment, 123-125
    concept of unity, 124-125
    continental integration needed,
        124
    early programs, 113-114
    element of African revolutionary
        thought, 10, 67, 84
    evolution, 108, 110-113
    factor in securing order, 10, 67,
        108-125
    and Houphouet-Boigny, 61
    and Kenyatta, 81
    linked with Arab socialism, 103
    and Nkrumah, 55, 77, 79, 99
    positive action phase, 112-113
    prospect of survival, 110
    and Senghor, 82
Pan-Arabism:
    and African socialism, 103
    and Bourguiba, 80
    and Nasser, 78-79
Pan-ism, preoccupying elites, 6
Parti-Démocratique de Guinée
    (PDG), 60
Political development:
    assessment difficult, 6, 9-10
    index of success, 9
    predicting, 5
    studies of non-West, 4-7
    viewed as precondition of
        economic development, 5
    by Western standards, 6
Political instability in early history
    of Non-West, 3
Political literature on Africa, 1-2, 3

Political modernization, requirements, 16

Political revolution, aim, 55

Portuguese colonial policy, 37

Poverty in Africa, 90

Power in African leaders, 61-65

Problems:
of modernization, 3
of present control, 92

Progress, 62
how to claim, 63
meaning for Africans, 35-36
socialism a factor in, 10, 66

Racism, 84, 130

Recent studies of Africa, 2

Religious base of African states, 31-35

Republic of South Africa, 18, 118, 121

Residual colonialism, 6

Revolutionary thought in Africa, 19, 47-67
Bourguiba's moderate, 58
Fanon an articulate exponent, 49-53

Rhodesia, 118, 121, 151-152

Ruanda-Burundi, 118

Russia, 19, 27, 105, 145
example of progress, 105
and Nasser, 102
non-West alert to domination, 130

Scholarship development in study of non-West, 2-10

Search for identity, 10

Second World War, 1-2, 15, 18-19, 24, 137

Security through neutralism, 10, 67, 128-142

Self-determination, 55

Senegal, 32, 44, 82-83, 116

Senghor, Léopold Sédar, 48, 79, 117
and democratic socialism, 44, 94
and nationalism, 82-83
and Pan-Africanism, 124

Social democracy, concept of Nasser, 5-7

Social discontinuity in early history of non-West, 3

Social revolution, aim, 55-56

Social sciences, revolution in approach, 3-4

Socialism, 66, 90-106
alternative pattern for change, 105
answer in Africa, 44-45, 48
answer to need, 90-91
defined by Kenyatta, 93-94
defined by non-West, 105
factor in progress, 10, 67
favored by non-West, 105
goal of AAPO, 115
"natural" to Africa, 104
principle of nationalist programs, 113
prospects in Africa, 103-106

Somalia, 26, 118, 152

Southwest Africa, 111, 118

Sovereignty:
anachronistic, 140
appealing to Africans, 140

Soviet Union (see Russia)

Successful political system, 9

Sudan, 32, 116, 153

Suez, 18, 102
conflict in, 24
nationalization of Canal, 154

Swaziland, 23, 118

Sylvester-Williams, Henry, 110

Tanganyika, 32, 111, 118, 119

Tanzania, 44, 58-59, 119 (see also Tanganyika)

Tensions in Africa, compared with previous international tensions, 153-154

Thermonuclear weaponry, 18, 24, 25

Tito:
influence on Nasser, 102
sponsor of Afro-Asian solidarity, 138

Togoland, 111, 151, 153

Totalitarianism, current social thought in Africa, 48

Touré, Ahmed Sékou, 48-49, 115, 116
and authoritarian socialism, 94

Touré, Ahmed Sékou *(Cont.)*
    exponent of unity, 121
    and militant Pan-Africanism, 122
    revolutionary principles, 59-60
    sponsor of Afro-Asian bloc, 138
Traditional communalism, basis of
    socialist system, 104
Tribal organization, 30-31, 75, 84
    effective support to leader, 30
    hindrance to political stability,
      30
    immovable object, 65
    individual liberty lacking in, 30
Triple sphere concept of Nasser, 56
Trusteeships, 111
Tubman, William, 117
Tunisia, 57-58, 79-80, 103, 152
"Tyranny of the weak," 27

UAMS, 116-118, 121
UAS, 116-118
Uganda, 32, 118
Underdevelopment of African states,
    2
Understanding non-West political
    development, 2-10
Union of African and Malagasy
    States (UAMS), 116-118, 121
Union of African States (UAS),
    116-118
United Arab Republic (UAR), 117
United Nations, 70, 116, 141
    African participation in, 133
    faith of African states in, 23
    membership, 23, 164-166
United States:
    and African studies, 4-8
    aid from, 135
    attitude of non-West toward, 148
    rivalry with Russia, 3

United States *(Cont.)*
    spirit of revolution conveyed by,
      19
Unity:
    nationalism, a sense of, 150
    Pan-African concept varies,
      124-125
Upper Volta, 116
USSR *(see* Russia)

Values:
    differing Western and non-
      Western, 1
    need for adapting, 42-45
Vietnam, 140

Warfare, change in trends, 24-25
West African Federation, 113, 151
Western world:
    aid from, 27, 135
    confronted with differing
      non-West, 1
    domination by, 130
    early model for emerging African
      states, 2
    effect of institutions on
      Africa, 19-22, 35-39, 85-86
    non-West committed to, 105,
      156-158
    political ideas not readily
      applicable to Africa, 43
    reaction to non-West states, 145
    standards currently rejected, 7
    techniques and African develop-
      ment, 29
World War II *(see* Second World War)

Zanzibar, 118

53-302

93587

DATE DUE

320.096   1968
S132a
Said, Abdul A
The African phenomenon.

OHIO DOMINICAN COLLEGE
LIBRARY
COLUMBUS, OHIO 43219

DEMCO